Open a Window to Your Soul

"You will see so much more beauty in the world and will wonder how you missed seeing it in the past."

—Richard Webster

When you are enthusiastic or excited, don't be surprised if a radiant yellow glow suddenly appears around you. Lose your temper, and a dirty red haze might hover around your body. Do something magnanimous and your aura will expand. Simply put, your aura is a physical manifestation of your soul.

Now you can learn to see the energy that emanates off yourself and other people through the proven methods taught by Richard Webster in his psychic training classes.

Learn to feel the aura, see the colors in it, and interpret what those colors mean. Explore the chakra system and how to restore balance to chakras that are over- or under-stimulated. Imprint your desires into your aura to attract what you want in your life. It's all possible with *Aura Reading for Beginners*.

About the Author

Richard Webster (New Zealand) travels around the world every year lecturing and conducting workshops on psychic subjects. His other books include *Feng Shui for Beginners*; *Revealing Hands*; *Omens, Oghams & Oracles*; and *Dowsing for Beginners*.

To Write to the Author

If you wish to contact the author or would like more information about this book, please write to the author in care of Llewellyn Worldwide and we will forward your request. Both the author and publisher appreciate hearing from you and learning of your enjoyment of this book and how it has helped you. Llewellyn Worldwide cannot guarantee that every letter written to the author can be answered, but all will be forwarded. Please write to:

Richard Webster
% Llewellyn Worldwide
P.O. Box 64383, Dept. K798-6
St. Paul, MN 55164-0383, U.S.A.

Please enclose a self-addressed stamped envelope for reply, or $1.00 to cover costs. If outside U.S.A., enclose international postal reply coupon.

Develop Your Psychic Awareness for
Health & Success

AURA
READING
for BEGINNERS

• •

Richard Webster

1998
Llewellyn Publications
St. Paul, Minnesota 55164-0383 U.S.A.

FIRST EDITION
First Printing, 1998

Cover design: Lisa Novak
Interior illustrations: Jeannie Ferguson (pages xiii, 18, 20, 23, 25, 26, 30, 32–34, 76, 77, 104, 131) and Tom Grewe (pages 6–8, 12, 13, 19, 66,)
Book design and editing: Michael Maupin

Library of Congress Cataloging-in-Publication Data
Webster, Richard, 1946 –
  Aura reading for beginners : develop your psychic awareness for health & success / Richard Webster. -- 1st ed.
      p.   cm.
  Includes bibliographical references and index.
  ISBN   1-56718-798-6
  1. Aura.   I. Title.
BF1389.A8W43   1998
133.8'92--dc21   97-32119
                                              CIP

Publisher's Note: Llewellyn Worldwide does not participate in, endorse, or have any authority or responsibility concerning private business transactions between our authors and the public.
   All mail addressed to the author is forwarded but, unless specifically instructed by the author, the publisher cannot give out an address or phone number.

Llewellyn Publications
A Division of Llewellyn Worldwide, Ltd.
P.O. Box 64383, Dept. K798-6
St. Paul, MN 55164-0383, U.S.A.

Dedication

For *Eden*, our first grandchild

Other Books by Richard Webster

Dowsing for Beginners
Feng Shui for Beginners
Omens, Oghams & Oracles
Revealing Hands
Seven Secrets to Success
Talisman Magic

Forthcoming

101 Feng Shui Tips for the Home

Contents

Introduction

As a child I went to a church school. Every Thursday morning we attended a chapel service before school began. I was very interested in music and always positioned myself so that I could watch Mr. Carder, the organist. He also taught music and was one of the best teachers I ever had.

One morning as I watched him playing Bach, I was amazed to see beautiful colors emanating from him and heading up towards the high, vaulted ceiling. I was fascinated by this sight and prodded the boy next to me.

"Look at the beautiful colors," I said.

The boy looked, but saw nothing. I can't remember what he said, but it was enough to stop me mentioning the colors to anyone else.

From that time on, I saw colors around Mr. Carder almost every time he played. I simply took it for granted that the colors would be there, and did not think it strange that I never saw colors around anyone else, not even the school padre.

Years later, after a lecture I gave, someone came up to me and suggested that the colors might have been reflections from the stained glass windows in the chapel. I thought it unlikely as I was familiar with the pretty patterns the windows made over the congregation on sunny mornings. Nevertheless, I went back to the chapel and checked. The organ was placed in such a position that it was impossible for the stained glass windows to reflect on the organist.

What I had seen was my very first aura. I was fortunate in that I saw colors from the very start. Most people begin by seeing an almost colorless "surround" and only gradually do the colors appear. Because I was a child I simply took the aura for granted, despite the comments of the boy who was sitting next to me. I did not analyze it or even think about it very often. Occasionally, I would see the aura around Mr. Carder in class when he was playing the piano. However, it was never visible when he was teaching.

A year or two later, he became my class teacher. His method of maintaining discipline in the class was to read to us every Friday afternoon if we had behaved during the week. The book he read was a favorite book from his own childhood, and he handled this old, battered book with reverence and love. The story was an exciting adventure, and our behavior in the classroom steadily improved, week by week, as it was much more fun to follow the latest installment of the story than it was to study mathematics. As he read, his aura would grow and surround him with brilliant colors.

Once I became a teenager I occasionally noticed auras around other people, usually when they were talking enthusiastically about something that interested them. However, it was always something that occurred randomly. I never set out to see auras, but was also not surprised when I did see one.

At the age of seventeen I attended a series of lectures at the Theosophical Society and discovered there was much more to the subject than I had previously realized. It surprised me to learn that most of the other attendees were working extremely hard to try to see something that I had been taking entirely for granted for half of my life. I wanted to interject and say that they were trying too hard, and should simply relax and let it happen, but was too shy and reserved.

I still believe that the best way to learn to see auras is to do so in a relaxed and playful manner. If you attempt the task with grim determination, all the fun disappears and it becomes almost impossible to succeed.

I had a striking example of this many years ago when I first began conducting psychic development classes. A lady in the class was desperate to see auras. Despite my admonition to have fun with the different exercises she would approach each one as if it were a matter of life and death. Her stress levels rose as different members of the class reported success and she could see nothing. She took the class notes home and left them in her living room. One evening her husband picked them up and read them. He had had a couple of drinks and thought it might be fun to try the exercises. His wife was skeptical as he had always expressed total disbelief in the subject. However, partly to humor him, she agreed and they did some of the exercises together. To her amazement, she discovered she could see auras easily. She was even more amazed that her husband could too. In fact, her husband was so frightened by the experience that it was many months before he would participate in any more experiments with her. The interesting thing about this story is that, in the class, this lady was determined to see auras, but couldn't. At home, enjoying a fun experiment to humor her husband, she succeeded easily.

In this book I have included all the exercises from my psychic development classes. If you practice them, in a spirit of fun, I am confident that you too will be able to see and interpret auras.

People have been able to see auras since time began. Many ancient rock carvings and paintings show people wearing a strange type of headgear. The drawings from the Val Camonica region in Northern Italy are particularly striking. Some authorities say that this proves we had visitors from outer space in the distant past. This is possible, of course, but it is more likely to be a crude depiction of an aura, particularly as some of these drawings show what appear to be flames surrounding the head. The headdresses worn by Native American chiefs could well depict the aura. The Mayan priests also wore plumed headdresses.

Holy people have been portrayed with luminous or golden auras from well before Christian times (see Figure A). These halos around the head have been found in ancient pictures from Egypt, India, Greece, and Italy and certainly depict auras.[1]

Figure A.
Halo in ancient pictures

Auras are also mentioned in the sacred books of every civilization. It seems highly likely that Moses' face was surrounded by a halo when he came down from the mountain. "He did not know that the skin on his face was radiant after speaking with Yahweh. And when Aaron and all the sons of Israel saw Moses, the skin on his face shone so much that they would not venture near him."[2] Homer described the aura as being "a luminous nebula derived from the divine essence, and so came to symbolize power."[3] Auras first appeared in Western writings some 2,600 years ago when the Pythagoreans began incorporating it in their teachings.[4]

People have considered the aura to be the true home of the life force since time began. The Hindus called this energy *prana*. In Polynesia, the Hunas called it *mana*. Paracelsus called it *munis*. Mesmer called it *animal magnetism*.[5] Baron von Reichenbach called it *od*, and today psychics call it the *etheric force*.

Medieval saints and mystics were able to see four different types of aura: the Nimbus, the Halo, the

Aureola, and the Glory. The first two surround the head, the Aureola surrounds the entire body and the Glory combines the other three into a single whole.[6] Obviously, saints and other holy people possess extremely powerful Nimbus and Halo auras, which were easily seen and portrayed by artists.

Paracelsus (1493–1541), the famous Swiss philosopher-physician, was one of the first people in the West to write about the aura. After graduating from university he traveled around Europe, spending a great deal of time with gypsies and alchemists. He also learned as much as he could about herbalism, dentistry, and theosophy. During this period he learned the information that later appeared in his writings. Paracelsus believed that there was a vital force that "radiates within and around living beings like a luminous sphere."[7] He regarded it as a magnetic influence that could be used to heal his patients. He was forced to resign his position as Professor of Medicine and Surgery in 1528 because his teachings were considered too unorthodox. Paracelsus died in 1541 from injuries he received after a servant of a physician who disagreed with his views pushed him from an upstairs window.

Sir Isaac Newton (1642–1727), the physicist and mathematician, is best remembered for watching an apple fall to the ground. Thinking about this enabled him to create his three fundamental laws of mechanics, which led to the Law of Gravitation. However, he was a multitalented man who worked in many spheres. As a mathematician he invented infinitesimal calculus. In science he discovered the composition of white light.

As a civil servant he was warden of the mint. In 1666, as a philosopher, he developed the concept of a force field or "waves of force" surrounding all living things. He was also the first person to pass white light through two prisms, which led to the laws of refraction and reflection. His "waves of force," plus his interest in color and light, make him an early pioneer in aura research.

Franz Mesmer (1734–1815), was a Viennese doctor who became fascinated with magnetism and used magnets to help cure his patients. He believed that a power similar to magnetism existed in the human body. He published his book *Dissertation on the Discovery of Animal Magnetism* in 1775 and began traveling widely to demonstrate his findings. Unfortunately, his theatrical approach and eccentricities antagonized the medical profession and, in 1784, a commission headed by Benjamin Franklin called him a quack and a charlatan.

The next important name in the history of the aura is Baron Karl von Reichenbach (1788–1869), the discoverer of *creosote*. Reichenbach was a German metallurgist and industrialist who became frustrated when his ideas were not accepted by others. Eventually, he decided to take his views directly to the public through a series of *Letters on Od and Magnetism*. "Od" is the name that Reichenbach used to describe a universal energy that he found sensitive people, particularly psychics, were in tune with. He believed that this "odic force" (named after Odin, one of the main gods of Norse mythology) was created by magnets, crystals, and human beings. Sensitive people could not only feel it, but in certain circumstances could see it. For instance, he found that his sensitives could feel a pleasant, cool sensation emanating from the top of a crystal, and an unpleasant, lukewarm feeling from the bottom.

In May 1844, he conducted tests with Angelica Sturmann, a young, gifted girl. She was placed in a dark room with a crystal and reported seeing a fine blue light streaming out of the top of the crystal. The light constantly moved and occasionally emitted sparks. When Reichenbach turned the crystal around, Angelica could see a dense yellow and red smoke coming from the bottom end. Reichenbach was delighted with this result. However, he was even more excited to discover that Angelica was just the first of thousands of people who later saw colors emanating from Reichenbach's crystals.[8] Reichenbach also discovered that the human body produces a polarity similar to that of crystals. He considered the left side of the body to be a negative pole and the right side positive.

In his numerous articles Baron von Reichenbach included many experiments for his readers to try. They created a sensation throughout Europe, with hundreds of thousands of people practicing to see his odic force. "Pray, test this for yourself," he said again and again to readers of his articles.[9]

Dr. Walter J. Kilner (1847–1920) broke new ground in 1908 when he discovered a process that enabled anyone to see the aura. His book *The Human Aura* was prophetic, because in it he pronounced his belief that in time the human aura could be photographed. Kilner's process for seeing auras involved a screen containing two plates of glass one-eighth of an inch apart. This space was filled with a solution of dicyanin, which is an indigo-violet colored dye. The resulting screen enabled people to see the ultra-violet range. Consequently, anyone looking through this screen was able to see auras. Kilner reported that the first person he looked at through the screen was a twenty-three year old woman who had a blue-gray aura with rays emanating from her body. Dr. Kilner was saddened by the response of the medical fraternity who laughed at his findings. In fact, in 1912 the British Medical Journal compared his findings with Macbeth's "visionary dagger."[10] Kilner believed that any doctor could use the screen as a diagnostic tool because unwell parts of the person's body showed up as a dark area in the aura. Despite his loss of reputation, Dr. Kilner continued with his experiments and his final book *The Human Atmosphere*[11] came out in 1921.

The next serious book on the subject of auras did not appear until 1937 when Oscar Bagnall's book *The Origin and Properties of the Human Aura* was published. He carried on from where Dr. Kilner had left off, and developed a screen containing pinacynol and methalene blue. The big advantage of Oscar Bagnall's screen was that it could be worn as spectacles. These "aura goggles" can still be purchased today.

In the late 1930s a Russian scientist named Semyon Kirlian accidentally discovered how to photograph the aura. He observed a tiny flash of light between a patient's skin and an electrode, when the patient was receiving shock treatment at a psychiatric institution.

Kirlian was burned when he first tried to photograph this light, but the photographic plate revealed an auric field and the pain was quickly forgotten.

Kirlian, with his wife Valentina, struggled on their own for more than twenty years, perfecting the process in their own time in their tiny two-room apartment. Word gradually spread about his discovery and finally the Russian Ministry of Public Health gave them a grant in the 1960s. The Kirlians conducted numerous experiments, including an interesting one where they were handed two identical looking leaves. Photographs were taken and one leaf produced a bright, flaring aura, but the other produced a feeble, weak aura. The first leaf was healthy, but the second was diseased.

Kirlian photographs are astonishingly beautiful, and when knowledge of them first reached the West, interest in parapsychology circles was extreme. However, the excitement gradually died down when scientists pointed out that the photographs were simply a *corona discharge*.[12] Whether or not this is actually the case is not yet known. Kirlian photography does not use a camera. The object being photographed is usually placed between two metal plates that oscillate by as much as 200,000 cycles a second. Photographs of fingers or hands are created by placing the part to be photographed against film that is sitting on a charged metal plate.

In 1953, Dr. Mikhail Kuzmich Gaikin, a Leningrad surgeon, read an article about the Kirlians. He was fascinated to find that their aura photographs reminded him when, as a surgeon in the Second World War, he watched Chinese doctors using acupuncture. These doctors told him about the 700 points on the skin where Vital Energy, or the Life Force, could be tapped. He watched these doctors change patients' energy flow on these points and effect cures. As he examined the aura photographs in the Kirlians' small office he became aware that the areas where the lights flashed most brilliantly matched up with the acupuncture points that the Chinese had known about for thousands of years.[13] This discovery made it much easier to detect the fine acupuncture points. In fact, Dr. Gaikin and Vladislav Mikalevsky, a Leningrad engineer, went on to invent an electronic device that can pinpoint an acupuncture position to within one tenth of a millimeter.[14]

In fact, the Kirlians were not the first to photograph auras. The Schlieren device, a nineteenth-century German invention to detect flaws in glass, also detects what may be auras, although scientists say that what it photographs are actually convection currents. Either way, both scientists and psychics now say that we are all surrounded by energies that are invisible to most people. In fact, scientists are now able to view auras on videotape, reporting that "a thin pulsating field was displayed around the human body."[15]

Today you can find people offering to photograph your aura at psychic fairs. Unfortunately, these cameras create an aura electronically, rather than photographing the actual aura. They usually work by attaching sensors to the skin of the person being photographed.

The electrical resistance that is measured is fed into an electronic processor which generates a pattern around the person. It is fun to have a photograph taken with one of these cameras, but the result is not a true photograph of your aura.

We have come a long way since primitive people drew auras on cave walls. Today we can use artificial devices to see the auras and effectively prove their existence. Despite this, very few people have been willing to spend the necessary time and energy to develop aura consciousness and become able to see auras whenever they wish.

Congratulations on starting an exciting and richly rewarding journey.

What Is the Aura?

• • • • • • • • • • • • • • • • • • • **1**

According to the dictionary, the aura is an invisible emanation or energy field that surrounds all living things. As there is an energy field around everything, even a rock or kitchen table has an aura. In fact, the aura, although it surrounds the entire body, is also part of every cell of the body and reflects all the subtle life energies. Consequently, it can be regarded as being simply an extension of the body, rather than something that surrounds it. The name *aura* comes from the Greek word *avra*, which means breeze. The energies flowing through our auras reflect our personalities, lifestyle, thoughts and emotions. Auras vividly reveal our mental, physical, and spiritual well-being.

Some people claim that the aura is simply an electro-magnetic phenomenon and should be ignored. Others believe that it consists of the spark of life and houses our higher consciousness, which provides the necessary energies for us to live and function. Still others consider the aura to be a reflection of ourselves, which consequently holds a complete record of our past and present, and even future. In fact, it is probably a combination of all of these.

Scientists agree that we all possess what is known as a physical aura. This is made of physical matter and energy fields that surround the body. As people are normally warm in relation to their surroundings, we all have thermal gradients with resulting air currents close to our bodies. Infrared energy is radiated from our bodies. We also have electrostatic and electrical ion fields surrounding us. As well as this, we emit low levels of electromagnetic radiation (radio waves) and low-frequency radiation of as much as one hundred kilocycles.[1]

However, the aura also contains color, and color is created from light. Sir Isaac Newton was the first to demonstrate this in 1666 when he observed the action of sunlight passing through a glass prism, creating a rainbow. This was a revolutionary discovery, as up until then everyone thought that color was an inherent part of every object. Like all people who are ahead of their time, Newton was ridiculed for his ideas. However, he persisted with his experiments and observed what happened when he passed light through two prisms. Light from the first prism divided up into a rainbow, but this rainbow turned back to a clear light after passing through the second prism. This effectively answered his critics' comments that the color was already inside the glass prism and sunlight simply picked up the color that was already there.

Sir Isaac Newton had discovered refraction. Light is refracted, or "bent" as it passes through the prism. Red is refracted less than the other colors as it has the longest wavelength. Violet has the shortest wavelength and is refracted most.[2] Although we term black and white as colors, they are in fact the opposite polarities of darkness and light, respectively. Sir Isaac Newton, of course, proved that white light contains every color.

Goethe described this very well when he wrote: "Colors are the sufferings of light." By that he meant that as the vibratory rhythm of white light is lowered, the different colors become visible.[3]

When light reaches the surface of an object, some of the colors are absorbed. The colors that are reflected back are the only ones that we are able to see. Consequently, a green leaf appears green to us because it has absorbed all the other colors.

Darker colors absorb more than lighter colors. This is why we tend to wear lighter colors in summer. I have a friend who wears nothing but black all year round. In summer he swelters, even though his clothing is made of lightweight material. This is because the black material is absorbing all the colors of the rainbow.

Light travels through space in the form of waves at 186,000 miles per second. Some of these waves are more than 100,000 miles in length, while others are microscopic. In the middle is the color spectrum, a small band of vibrant energy that we can see.

It was not until 1676 that the Danish astronomer, Olaf Roemer, discovered the velocity of light. This was a revolutionary concept at the time. Up until this discovery it was believed that light simply existed and did not need time to travel.[4]

It is intriguing, then, to realize that our auras are not composed of some form of light. This is a common misconception, for although scientific instruments nowadays can detect every part of the light spectrum, they are unable to detect auras. Our ability to see them is a type of clairvoyance. There is no need to let this worry you though, as it is a perfectly natural ability that we all have.

In the 1960s, John Ott, a leading light researcher, discovered that the eye serves two completely different functions. As light enters the eye it is transmitted to the brain through the optic nerve. This allows us to see. John Ott found that light is also received by a nucleus of cells in the retina of the eye which transmit the information to the hypothalamus. The hypothalamus is a small prune-shaped knob at the base of the brain which controls a number of important functions, such as our sense of balance, sex drive, weight and stress levels. It also controls the pituitary gland, which in turn influences all the endocrine glands. John Ott theorized that light being sent to the pituitary must consequently be affecting our growth and health at an unconscious level.[5] This discovery has important applications in color healing and determining health in the aura.

Although auras are not created by light, light is necessary to see them. Auras grow and expand in sunlight and shrink when indoors. Obviously, they shrink even more in total darkness. They do not completely disappear though, and can be seen as small, fine bluish lines of energy. As a child I used to enjoy going under the bed clothes and placing my fingertips close together to watch the fine lines of energy dancing between them.

Throughout history, certain people have been able to see auras. However, it is only in recent times that scientists have been able to verify the existence of this invisible "surround" that psychic people have always been able to see.

In fact, many people are able to see auras as children, but lose the ability as they mature. My experience of suddenly seeing the aura around the music teacher at school is not an uncommon one with children, and as a child I simply took the experience for granted. It is only as we get older and learn that these things are supposedly impossible that we lose the ability. Fortunately, many parents and teachers are more enlightened today than they were a few decades ago, and encourage psychic potential in children. However, there is still a long, long way to go in this regard.

You will find as you develop your awareness of auras that you will spontaneously see other people's auras from time to time. Usually, there will be a reason for this. You may unexpectedly see someone you care about and, because you are elated at seeing your friend, suddenly see his or her aura. It may even serve as a warning if you suddenly see someone with a murky aura. If someone suddenly loses their temper, you are quite likely to see a dirty red auric haze suddenly appear around them. If someone does something magnanimous or generous, their aura is likely to expand and become highly visible for a short period of time. At a party I went to many years ago I experienced the sad situation of suddenly noticing the aura of someone on the far side of the room. His aura was weak and tired, telling me that he was unwell. Two days later he died. I wondered for a long time why I suddenly saw his aura when I was not seeing any other aura in the room. I feel now that his aura was signaling the fact that he was about to move on to another incarnation.

Auras are seen in different ways. Usually, they are seen as energy fields that totally surround the body like a huge egg (Figure 1.1). In fact, many people have described the aura as being an "auric egg."[6] Most auras extend several feet around the body. It is believed that the more spiritually evolved the person is, the larger his or her aura will be. The aura of the Buddha, for instance, was believed to have extended for several miles. Inside this large egg are lines

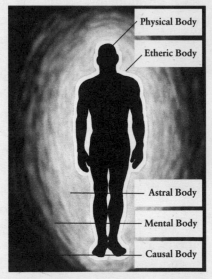

Figure 1.1. Aura energy fields

of force and energy, radiating in all directions and reflecting the person's thought processes, feelings, health and potentials (Figure 1.2).

Auras are made up of energy fields that flow at right angles to each other. The first flows up and down the body in a vertical direction. At right angles to this are energy fields that flow around the body in a horizontal direction. Finally, other waves of energy emanate from the spine and head towards

Figure 1.2. Radiating energy in aura

the outer extremities of the aura. They all crisscross and create a mesh of interwoven magnetic energy.

Auras consist of different layers. Some psychics are able to see several layers (known as subtle bodies), and most people with training are able to see at least three.[7] In traditional interpretation each layer of the aura represented a different area of life. For instance, the mental aura governed the thought processes and the astral aura the emotions. However, in our daily lives we usually act with a mixture of these. We still use our emotions when we think, and even when acting emotionally, some thought is still involved. Nowadays, we are aware that everything is interwoven and integrated together and consequently, we tend to look at the aura as a whole.

The sole exception is the etheric double. This is an extremely fine, almost invisible surround that extends between a quarter and half an inch all around the body (Figure 1.3). It expands during sleep and contracts during the waking hours. It seems to work as a battery that recharges itself overnight.

When people first develop auric sight they see the etheric double as a space between the physical body and the aura proper. However, as their sight develops

Figure 1.3. Etheric double

they become aware that the etheric double has a grayish tinge, yet constantly shimmers, moves, and changes color. This constant movement inside the etheric double creates a wide variety of almost luminous colors that are delicate and constantly changing. The etheric double is sometimes known as the health aura, as illnesses can be seen here as a dark smudge or a break in the movements of the aura. Ultimately, the area resembles a dark, stagnant pool inside the etheric double. Ill health can also be determined by a loss of coloration in the etheric double. This is probably why it is so often described as being gray in color. Interestingly enough, ill health can usually be determined before the person is aware that anything is wrong. If people are aware of this, they can take steps to restore their health and vitality before anything disastrous happens. It is not surprising that many spiritual healers work on the etheric double.

A friend of mine who used to be a heavy smoker gave up the habit when he was told that his aura was gray. Within weeks his aura returned to its former brilliance. If he had carried on smoking he would have become very ill, as his aura was exhibiting a clear warning of potential ill health.

Even our thoughts can affect the etheric double. If we constantly think negative or hostile thoughts, these will ultimately be visible inside the etheric double. Positive thoughts and actions likewise have a beneficial effect on our health and well-being, and this is also reflected in a beautiful etheric double.

Surrounding the etheric body is the aura proper. Some people see this as a number of separate sheaths. In fact, in the East the term *koshas* is used to describe these, and this word means "sheath."[8] The aura extends for several feet and it can sometimes be felt and seen by people who have no knowledge or interest in psychic subjects. With training, anyone can learn to feel and see the aura. The aura appears to expand in both size and vibrancy in sunlight, and this is probably why we feel more alive and energetic in summer than we do in winter.

When the aura is first seen it appears to be white and almost cloud-like in appearance. Gradually, as auric sight develops, colors can be seen. Every aura has a basic color that reveals important information about the person. This color shows the person's emotional, mental, and spiritual nature.

As well as this, the aura contains rays of different colors that emanate from the body and radiate outwards through the aura. Some people consider these to be thought waves, and certainly our thoughts and emotions influence our auras enormously. This is doubtless where common sayings such as "red with rage" and "green with envy" come from. These thought waves come and go, and are not to be considered a permanent part of the aura. No one remains "red with rage" for weeks or months on end. However, negative thoughts and emotions can create permanent changes in the aura. In these instances, they change the naturally glorious, vibrant colors of the aura into dull, repulsive, even evil-looking colors.

A few people have a variety of geometrical shapes and forms inside their auras, and they are believed to have symbolical significance. For instance, a circle inside the aura is a symbol of fulfillment and inner contentment. A triangle is a sign that a person protects others, or that someone is protecting them. A star indicates significant psychic ability.

In addition, you will sometimes see arrows, coils, cones, crosses, crescents, and a variety of other shapes and designs inside people's auras. Arrows frequently appear when the person is under stress or strain, particularly if it has been going on for a long period of time. Crosses indicate reluctance to make a decision, and are most frequently found in the auras of indecisive, timid people. Coils, cones and crescents are usually an indication of serious thought, and are often found with thought forms. Interestingly enough, they are seldom found in the auras of people who have mentally stimulating occupations. You will find them mainly in the auras of people who for some reason or other are presently using their brains more than usual. I have noticed this several times in the auras of people who are becoming spiritually aware, but are trying to reason it out logically.

Some of these shapes and forms may well be thought forms. When this is the case, you will notice that they last for several seconds and then disappear. This is because most of us cannot sustain a single thought for any length of time. Usually, they are symbols from our minds and these can last for months, years or even a lifetime. You normally see these in intellectuals and spiritually evolved people.

Our auras are reacting with other people's auras all the time. When we meet someone we like, our auras open up and allow the two auras to mingle (Figure 1.4). When two people who are deeply in love are together their auras often seem to combine to create one, large, gloriously vibrant aura (Figure 1.5). When we meet someone we do not like, the auras repel each other (Figure 1.6). Have you ever met someone you instantly disliked, yet you could think of no reason for this antipathy? Your aura would have been repelled by the other person's aura, warning you to keep away from this person. Consequently, someone who is always thinking negative thoughts will gradually repel everyone who comes into his or her life.

A few people are "psychic vampires," draining your aura energy to enhance their own. Have you ever felt

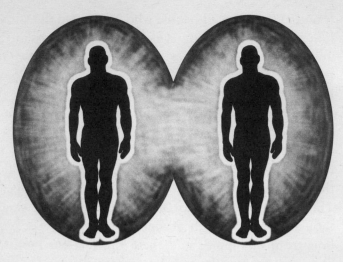

Figure 1.4. Auras mingle

totally drained of energy after spending time with someone? The chances are that person was a psychic vampire. These unfortunate people are usually rigid in outlook, psychically unaware, and lacking in self-esteem. Consciously or unconsciously they drain energy from other people, which works out well for them but leaves everyone else feeling depleted and frustrated. If you are living with a psychic vampire, you need to learn how to protect your aura.

Negative thinking is also bad. I know someone who has done very well in his chosen career, achieving prominence and a small amount of fame. Yet he feels that he is not given the respect and deference that he deserves. He has gradually become more and more bitter about this, and this is clearly reflected in the murky nature of his aura. Not surprisingly, people go

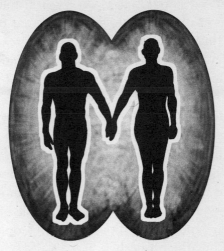

Figure 1.5. Auras combine

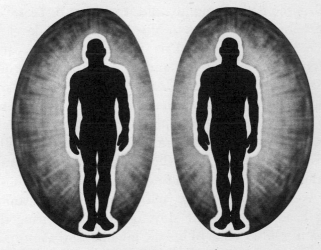

Figure 1.6. Auras repel

out of their way to avoid him, and this makes him even more negative. He is on a spiral that is leading him into a sad, lonely old age. Yet he has the power to change this. If he would let go of the real and imagined grievances of his past, and live happily from day to day, his aura would change to reflect his new reality, and he would then attract people to him again.

The aura is not present at birth, but with the first intake of breath the very beginnings of the aura can be seen.[9] This appears to indicate that the aura consists of energy that is absorbed into the system by the breath and then radiated out again in the form of the aura. Further evidence of this is the noticeable improvement in the sizes and colors of the auras of people who exercise and breathe properly.

A baby's aura is virtually colorless, but by the time he or she is three months old it appears to be silver. This gradually changes to blue, denoting the development of intelligence. This is especially noticeable between the ages of one and two years. As the child grows, so does the aura. It gradually develops in size and brilliance, revealing the child's potentials, and his or her ultimate colors. The blue remains as a background color inside the aura throughout the child's life. It is usually noticed only when the person is ill, because it then develops a grayish tinge which is very obvious.

As the baby grows, a yellow haze appears around the head, denoting the start of thought. During the first five or six years of life the infant absorbs information like a sponge. As he or she continues to learn, the yellow brightens and becomes more intense.

By the time the child starts formal education his or her aura will be reflecting the true colors that will be worn throughout life.

The aura should be radiant with colors that are intense and almost luminous in appearance. However, our characters alter our auras in many subtle ways. For instance, a generous person will have a large aura with colors that appear to be drawn in pastels. A miser, on the other hand, will have an aura that is small and murky in appearance, as if the colors have been slightly muddied.

Average people possess average auras and the intensity and size depends entirely on their mood at the time. If they are feeling generous their auras appear strikingly beautiful. However, when they are contemplating something that might be underhanded or dishonest their auras contract and become murky.

Auras are at their most gorgeous when people are in love. Their auras expand and the colors dance vibrantly. When the two lovers are together their auras merge into one, creating a single aura that reaches heavenwards.

Genuinely good, kind people also possess large, beautiful auras. Many of these people are taken for granted by their families, but spend their lives quietly helping others and doing good deeds which may or may not be noticed and appreciated.

As you can see, the ability to see the aura can be extremely useful and practical. It can tell you when you are in the presence of someone who is generous, loving and kind, and it can also warn you of someone who is dishonest, lustful or wanting to take advantage of you in some other way. The rest of this book will tell you how to feel, see, and interpret auras.

• • • • • • • • • • • • • • • • • • • 2

Feeling the Aura

Many people discover they can see auras spontaneously, but most people have to learn how to develop their auric sight. In my psychic classes I found it was better for my students to learn how to feel auras before attempting to see them.

You will need someone to experiment with. Ideally, this will be someone who is also wanting to develop his or her psychic abilities. It is a waste of time doing these experiments with people who do not believe in auras, as they will quickly get bored and their negativity will adversely affect you. Choose someone who is open-minded and positive in outlook. I have found that friends are usually better than family members, as family members can sometimes help out of a sense of duty, rather than wanting to. Some people say that it is easier to see women's auras than men's.[1] I have not noticed this myself, and feel that the most important thing is to choose someone who you like and who is a feeling, as well as logical, person.

Dowsing the Aura

It is helpful to have some idea of the size of the aura before starting to feel for it. Later on we will feel the aura with our hands, but a good first test is to use two angle rods and dowse for it. Dowsing is usually used to locate something that is hidden below the surface of the earth.[2] Water divining is a good example. However, it can be used for many other purposes. Some people feel that dowsing is a strange, mysterious, even superstitious practice. In fact, it is an extremely practical way of getting in contact with your subconscious mind.

First of all you will need to make yourself a pair of angle rods (Figure 2.1). These are simply two L-shaped pieces of metal. The longer side should be ten to twelve inches long, and the shorter side about six inches in length. I made my first set from two wire coat hangers.

Figure 2.1. Dowsing angle rods

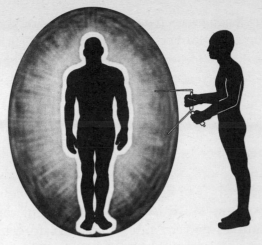

Figure 2.2. The dowsing response

These angle rods are held loosely in your fists with the two longer sections facing directly in front of you. You may find it useful to place the shorter sections inside plastic straws to allow the rods to move freely inside your fists. I find that it works equally as well for me without the straws, but many people are inclined to grip the rods too firmly. Naturally, when they do this the rods cannot move freely.

Before dowsing for your friend's aura take the angle rods outside and dowse for the water mains that enter your property. Relax your mind as much as possible. Think to yourself that you are dowsing for water and then slowly walk from one side of your property to the other. At some stage the angle rods will start to cross over each other and will probably end up parallel to each other in front of you (Figure 2.2).[3] This is known as the dowsing response. It may seem uncanny at first. The key to success is to suspend disbelief and relax.

A few people experience the dowsing response in a different way. Rather than crossing over each other, the rods move outwards, away from each other. This makes no difference and is still a dowsing response.

Once you have experienced the sensation you will be able to repeat it whenever you wish. Now it is time to dowse your friend's aura. Ask your friend to stand with his or her legs and arms slightly spread. Stand about thirty feet away with your dowsing rods pointing forward. Think in general terms about your friend's aura. Move forward slowly until the angle rods start to move. Pause, and move forward even more slowly until the rods cross over. This indicates the outer edge of your friend's aura (Figure 2.3).

Make a mental note of this position, and then repeat the exercise from the other side. You will find your friend's aura extends an equal distance on each side. Now move slowly around your friend in a circle and watch the tips of your angle rods. You will find that your friend's aura is a perfect circle.

Figure 2.3. Dowsing aura outer edge

You are likely to be surprised at just how large your friend's aura is. This is because you are dowsing the outer edge of the aura. When you feel for the aura you may find that you are actually feeling one of the inner layers, rather than the outermost one.

Now it is time to start feeling your friend's aura.

Choose a time when you will not be interrupted. It might pay to take the phone off the hook. The room should be warm and you might wish to play some gentle meditation music. Begin by sitting down in a comfortable chair with your eyes closed.

Imagine the most peaceful scene that you can remember. It might be a gently flowing stream, or a beautiful sunset. It makes no difference what it is, just as long as you find it peaceful and relaxing.

Become aware of your breathing, and take three deep breaths, exhaling slowly. Then consciously relax the muscles in your toes and feet. Once you feel they are completely relaxed, think about the muscles in your calves and thighs. Gradually relax all the muscles in your body, until you feel loose, limp and totally relaxed.

There is no time limit on this. For the first few times you may find it difficult to relax completely, but after a while you will be able to do it in under a minute. In fact, people who have learned self-hypnosis can do it in a matter of seconds.

The purpose of this exercise is to open up the right-hand side of your brain. This is the nonverbal, feeling, intuitive side that you use whenever you are doing something creative. Many people spontaneously see auras when they are engaged in painting, gardening, playing music, or any other activity that engages the right-hand side of their brains.

Once you are totally relaxed, simply concentrate on your breathing. Imagine the oxygen coming into your lungs and being carried to every part of your body. Picture yourself as a perfect human being. It does not matter if you are overweight or in ill health. Simply picture yourself, in your mind's eye, as a perfect physical specimen. See yourself as being absolutely perfect in every way, a child of the universe. Feel proud of yourself. Think of some of your achievements, of your intelligence and creativity. Then think how your life will change once you are able to see and read auras.

Now, slowly stretch and open your eyes. The purpose of this relaxation exercise is to allow you to let go of all the problems and worries of your everyday life. It is very beneficial for you physically, as well, as every single muscle and organ in your body totally relaxes while doing this exercise. We should experience this every night during sleep, but often we don't. Have you ever awakened in the morning feeling tired and lacking energy? Although you were asleep, parts of your body were still tense. After doing the relaxation exercise you should feel alive and full of energy. This will be reflected in your aura.

You are now ready to start feeling auras. Rub the palms of your hands together briskly for several seconds and then hold them about twelve inches apart. You may feel some energy between them, particularly in the center of the palm and the tips of the fingers (Figure 2.4).

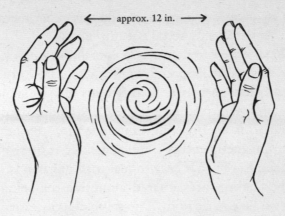

Figure 2.4. Energy between palms

Slowly bring your hands towards each other. You will gradually notice a very slight resistance as the auras from each hand meet. You may find it helpful to imagine that you are squashing a rubber ball between your hands. People experience this feeling in different ways. It may appear to be a slight resistance, or a tingling sensation, or even a feeling of warmth or coolness.

Continue bringing your hands together. You will suddenly notice the resistance subside as the aura from each hand merges with the other.

Hold your hands together for a few moments, and then slowly draw them apart. You will notice a fine coolness on your palms and fingertips as the auras separate again.

Experiment at this point by moving your hands a couple of inches towards and away from each other. You will notice the resistance as they move together, and the coolness as they move apart. You are feeling your own aura! Once you can do this experiment with ease, you are ready to take it further.

We all have seven energy points in our body known as chakras (see Chapter 5, Figure 5.1). These are nerve centers that absorb and distribute physical, mental, emotional and spiritual energies. The chakras are powerhouses of energy and, consequently, our personal electromagnetic energy is much greater at these points. As a result, they are easy to feel with our hands.

The chakras are situated alongside the spinal column in the etheric body. The seven chakras are:

1. *Root chakra*, situated at the base of the spine.
2. *Sacral chakra*, situated halfway between the pubic bone and the navel.
3. *Solar chakra*, situated at the level of the solar plexus.
4. *Heart chakra*, situated between the shoulder blades in line with the heart.
5. *Throat chakra*, situated at the level of the throat.
6. *Brow chakra*, situated at the level of the forehead, just above the eyebrows.
7. *Crown chakra*, situated at the top of the head.

It is an interesting test to locate all of your chakras by using your hands to feel for them. Once you find them, you will be surprised that you have never felt the energy emanating from them before.

For our next experiment use one of your hands to detect and feel the heart chakra. Again, hold your hand about twelve inches in front of your body and slowly bring it closer and closer to your chest. When you feel a slight resistance, draw your hand away until the resistance goes and then bring it slowly forward again until you feel the definite barrier created by your aura.

Now do this again but bring your hand towards a position on your body that is a few inches away from the heart chakra. Notice that your hand will get closer to your body before you feel any resistance. This is because the chakras create so much more

Figure 2.5.
Feeling the aura

energy than other areas, and are easier to locate.

Once you have successfully felt the aura around your heart chakra, try locating and feeling the aura around the other chakra positions. You will find, with practice, that the aura almost feels solid, and you will be amazed that you never felt it before. This is a good sign as it means that you are developing aura awareness.

Hopefully, your partner will be at a similar stage and be able to successfully feel his or her own aura.

We will now take a large leap forward and feel someone else's aura. Have your friend sit comfortably in a chair. Stand behind him or her and hold your hands about twelve inches away from each side of his or her head. Slowly bring them closer until you feel a resistance (Figure 2.5). Test it by moving your hands back and forth. Often your friend will feel the sensation on his or her aura at the exact moment you make contact with it.

Once you have felt it, move your hands in different directions to see if you can follow the aura around your friend's body.

After you have experimented with this a number of times, ask your friend to lie down comfortably on a bed with his or her eyes closed. Your task is to locate each of the chakras and

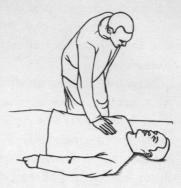

Figure 2.6.
Feeling the chakras

your friend will tell you when he or she feels your hand over a chakra position. The less clothing your partner is wearing, the easier this experiment is (Figure 2.6).

If you have practiced the previous experiments you will find it an easy matter to locate your friend's chakras. At the same time, your friend will be developing greater aura awareness, by identifying which chakra you are feeling with his or her eyes closed.

This experiment provides graphic evidence that you are both on the right track. With practice, your friend will be able to tell you which chakra you are over, at the very instant you locate it.

Naturally, after experimenting for a while, change roles so that you are lying with your eyes closed while your friend locates your chakras.

There is a final experiment in feeling auras before we move on to seeing them.

As you know, we all have our own personal body space and we dislike people intruding into it. Generally speaking, the more intimate we are with someone, the closer they can come into our personal space. When someone we hardly know or do not like enters our personal space we tend to move away. This is why people from different countries often have problems when they travel. For instance, someone from the Far East has a smaller personal space than the average American. Consequently, the visitor from the Far East would cause the American to back across the room by constantly and unwittingly entering the American's personal space. Dr. Charles Tart calls this personal space our "psychological aura."[4]

The exact same thing happens with our auras. When we are forced into close contact with someone we do not know, our auras are likely to repel the other person's aura. A good example would be a crowded underground commuter train where people are forced to stand close against people they do not know. In this situation, everyone's aura tends to contract and repel everyone else's. Next time you are forced into a crowded train or elevator see if you can feel the auras of the people surrounding you. It is possible to do this simply by being aware. You do not need to use your hands. In fact, that might not be desirable in this sort of situation!

If we like someone, our auras tend to open and allow the aura of our friend to intermingle with ours.

This final experiment allows you to test this. Ask your friend to stand on one side of the room. You stand on the other side, facing the wall, with your hands and legs spread out. Your friend has to approach you as quietly as possible, and your task is to determine when he or she has entered into your aura.

Your first attempts will be the most difficult. This is because your whole body will be extremely aware that your friend is approaching, and you may subconsciously imagine that he or she is closer than is actually the case. Do not worry about any failures. Stay relaxed and think pleasant thoughts. Ignore any sounds you may hear inside or outside the room. I always concentrate on my breathing and try not to let any other thoughts enter my mind. That way, when my friend gets close enough to contact my aura I am instantly aware of it.

This test is not as easy as it sounds. Because you are doing this with a friend, your auras will tend to intermix and you will not feel him or her breaking the barrier to the extent that you would with a stranger. I noticed this frequently with my psychic development classes. People who did not know each other were always more successful at this than people who were good friends. However, once I separated the friends and had them repeat the experiment with people they did not know, they were just as successful as everyone else.

You will not complete all these tests in an evening or even in a week. It is better to have several short sessions, rather than one lengthy one. You will also progress more quickly if you undertake these experiments with a feeling of playfulness. If you attempt them with a feeling of grim determination, you are most unlikely to be successful and will give up in disgust.

Once you can do all of these experiments successfully, you are ready to move on and learn how to see auras.

How to See Auras

3

By experimenting with the different tests in Chapter Two you will have developed your aura consciousness, making it much easier for you to learn to see auras. In fact, you may even have started seeing auras while feeling for them. Even if this is the case, you will still find it beneficial to work through the experiments in this chapter.

I found several of the students in my classes were able to mentally tune in and determine the color of the aura by feeling it. This is fascinating, and is similar to many clairvoyants who are able to intuitively sense colors without actually seeing them. However, even if you find you can intuitively sense the colors, practice the exercises in this chapter as it is much more convenient to be able to actually see the auras in their full splendor. Many authorities say that the colors of the aura are seen through the third eye, rather than through the eyes. This is impossible to answer, and sometimes I feel that I am picking up the colors intuitively, rather than through my eyes. However, I am still actually seeing the colors, rather than feeling them.

Start by sitting down somewhere comfortable and going through the relaxation exercise. When you feel you are sufficiently relaxed, both in your body and mind, open your eyes and try this first experiment.

Ensure that the lighting in the room is soft, rather than dim. Sit so that any bright lights are behind you. You do not want any light shining or reflecting into your eyes.

Place the tips of your forefingers together and look at them for about ten seconds. Then slowly move them apart. You will notice a fine, almost invisible thread of energy that stretches and keeps the fingertips joined, even though you are moving them slowly away from each other (Figure 3.1). The first time you do this, you may find this link disappears once your fingers are half an inch apart. However, with practice, you will find that the link remains visible to you even when your fingertips are four or five inches apart.

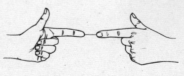

Figure 3.1

If you have any difficulties in seeing this line of energy, experiment by dimming the lights and holding your fingers over a light-colored surface. A sheet of white paper works well for most people, but a few prefer a darker background as they see this stream of energy as being almost white in color.

Once you are able to see it, you will find that you can see these threads of energy at any time, under any circumstances.

Now you can try the experiment again with all four fingers touching the fingers of the other hand. As you move your hands apart you will notice streams of energy joining all the fingers.

If your partner is doing this experiment at the same time, try to see the streams of energy joining his or her fingertips. It is exciting to see someone else's aura for the first time.

Now you can try something extremely interesting. Using the fingertips from one hand, touch the fingertips of your friend's hand, and then slowly separate them. You will notice the stream of pure energy joining you and your friend's fingertips. What do you think would happen if you were to do this experiment with someone you disliked? In fact, if possible, try this experiment with as many people as possible.

One very good way of doing this is to try the following experiment at a social gathering. It works best on a circular table with a dark surface, but any table will do. Seat everyone around the table and ask them to place both their hands on the table top with their fingers pointing towards the center. Dim the lights. Ask everyone to relax and try to see a fine network of lines crossing the table joining all the fingertips.

It may take five minutes for anyone to see anything, but once one person sees it, suddenly everyone else will,

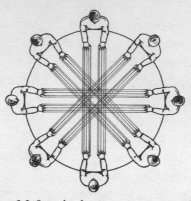

Figure 3.2. Strands of energy crisscrossing table

too. It is a stunningly beautiful effect, creating a cat's cradle of interweaving strands of energy crisscrossing the table (Figure 3.2). Once this experiment has been conducted, everyone in the room will have questions and be interested in doing the fingertip touching exercise with you.

You will find that the streams of energy stretch much farther when you do the exercise with some people than they do with others. This is because your aura reaches out to encompass the auras of people you like, but can do the exact opposite with people you do not enjoy being with.

Now you are ready to start seeing more of your own aura. You will need a room with a plain-colored wall, ideally white or cream. Dim the lights and stand several feet away from this wall, facing it. Extend your right arm out in front of you and raise your hand so the fingers are pointing towards the ceiling (Figure 3.3). Look at the wall, through the fingers of this hand. Focus on the wall, rather than your hand. You will notice after a few moments that your hand has a distinct aura around it. It will appear to be a gray, almost colorless haze.

Figure 3.3

Once you can see it, focus on this haze, rather than the wall. You may find it disappears when you do this. If this happens, simply gaze at the wall again until it reappears. Once you can see the aura clearly when you focus on it, look at the fingertips. You may see fine streams of energy radiating away from your fingertips. If you look closely at the aura surrounding your hand you will notice that it is constantly moving.

Some people express disappointment when they first see their own aura, as it appears almost colorless. Do not worry if this happens to you. The colors will start appearing later, once you become used to seeing the aura.

Experiment with your other hand, and then try the test again under other lighting conditions. A dim light is best when you are first learning, but in time you should be able to see auras under every type of lighting condition.

Experiment, also, by looking at other parts of your body. Once you can see the aura around your hand, you will find it easy to see the aura around every part of your body. Clothing restricts and constricts auric sight, so you may find it best to experiment nude or semi-clothed. Unfortunately, it is impossible for most people to see auras through a mirror. For some reason mirrors do not reflect auras well. However, a few people are able to see their own auras this way and you may find it interesting to experiment with your bathroom mirror.[1]

If you wear glasses, try looking at your aura with your glasses both on and off. I have found that many people who normally wear glasses are able to see auras more easily without them on.

Now it is time to experiment again with your partner. Ask your friend to stand in front of the plain-colored wall. Stand back several feet and look in the direction of your friend but focus on the wall behind him or her (Figure 3.4). The ideal state is almost like a daydream, where your eyes are open, but you are not really seeing anything. However, in this case, you are relaxing and concentrating at the same time. You might find it helpful to think about a time when you felt really tired and your eyes just

Figure 3.4

wanted to close. Naturally, you don't want your eyes to close now, but it can be helpful to think about such a time as your eyes will feel the necessary heaviness and automatically create the almost unfocused gaze.

It may feel strange when it happens, but suddenly you'll notice a hazy aura completely encircling your friend. You will see this with your peripheral vision.

You may find that the aura is solely around your friend's head and neck. This is because clothing constricts the aura and makes it much harder to see. Also, the considerable mental energy emanating from the head makes the aura in this part of the body easier to see.

Try focusing on this aura, once you see it. It is quite likely to disappear the first few times you try this, but be persistent. Once you can focus on it and still see it, observe it closely. You will find it constantly shifts and moves. You are also likely to find that it disappears for a moment or two after you blink.

Step closer and try touching it. It may take several attempts before you can both see and touch it at the same time. Most people find that the aura disappears as soon as they step forward to touch it. This is because the focus of their eyes change as they move forwards. When this happens, simply go back to where you were standing and start again. The aura should reappear in just a few seconds.

When you touch the aura you will feel the same sensations that you felt when you were doing the feeling exercises in the previous chapter, but now you will be able to see it as well. Notice how the aura initially moves away from the pressure of your fingers, but then allows your fingers to enter it. It is a little like pressing the surface of a balloon, the difference being that you can actually move through the surface and reach inside the aura.

Feel the aura in different parts of your friend's body. Pay particular attention to the chakras and notice how the aura moves in a rapid circular motion at these positions.

Now step back again to your original position and keep looking at the aura as you ask your friend to think of something that makes him or her angry. Observe any changes in the aura. It is likely to shrink slightly and you may notice some changes in coloration. Anger reveals itself as a dirty, reddish tinge in the aura.

Tell your friend to take several deep breaths and then think of something extremely happy. Watch the aura swell and expand.

Then, ask him or her to think of something neutral, neither sad nor happy, and watch the aura return to its normal size.

Finally, ask your friend to think of an experience that was either sad, angry, happy or neutral. You should be able to tell your partner what emotion he or she is thinking, purely by observing the aura.

Repeat some of these exercises outdoors. Make sure that the sun is behind you. Early morning or late in the afternoon are the best times to do these experiments. You will notice that your friend's aura will expand outdoors in the fresh air.

There are several other methods you can use to see the aura. Another similar method is to stare at your friend's forehead (rather than at the wall, as we did before). Concentrate on his or her forehead, and then gradually expand your peripheral vision, first to the left and right, then above and below. You will find that when your peripheral vision is extended as far as it will go in every direction, your eyes become slightly unfocused and a faint haze will appear around your friend's head. Keep your peripheral vision extended and after a few moments you will find this haze transformed into a distinct aura. Once it is clear, you will be able to focus on the aura. When you first attempt this, it is likely that the aura will disappear as soon as you focus on it. Simply do the exercise again (and again if need be) until you are able to focus clearly on the aura.

This final method is a combination of both previous methods. Again, your friend must stand or sit in front of a plain-colored wall. Stand several feet away and look at your friend's nose. See how far you can see with your peripheral vision above and to the left of your friend. Make a mark on the wall at that position. Return to your former position and repeat the exercise, this time locating a position above and to the right of your friend. Again make a mark, or stick something on the wall at that position. Repeat twice more to locate the positions below and to the left and right of your friend's nose. Start by staring at the mark you made above and to the left of your friend. After several seconds, quickly focus on the mark that is to the left and below your friend. Stare at this for several seconds and then shift your gaze to the mark that is below and to the right. Finally, stare at the mark that is above and to the right. After staring at this one for several seconds, allow your peripheral vision to gradually expand to include the three other positions that you had focused on. As you do this, your friend's aura will appear. As with the other versions, you may have to do this several times before you can focus your gaze directly on the aura.

Now it is time to celebrate your success so far. Take your friend to a shopping mall or some other place that is likely to be busy. Walk several paces behind your friend and see if you can see his or her aura in this distraction-filled environment.

Do not be disappointed if you cannot see it. A busy shopping mall is a totally different environment to a dimly lit, quiet room at home. Change places and see if your friend can see your aura.

Also look for auras around other people in the mall. There is no need to stare to do this. Simply focus several feet beyond them and try to see their auras with your peripheral vision. It is easiest when people have a clear background behind them. You will usually see the aura most clearly around their heads. However, if it is summer and people are scantily clad you will see auras around much of their bodies. It can be an overwhelming feeling to suddenly see auras around everyone. However, this usually takes time. The good thing is that you can practice wherever you are.

4

The Aura Colors

We all react emotionally to color. Even people who know nothing whatsoever about color instinctively know that warm colors create excitement and positive feelings, while cool colors relax people and create feelings of peace and tranquillity.

Even small children are able to give emotions and feelings to different colors. They usually relate red to anger, aggression and excitement, while green relates to peace, quietness and solitude.[1] A 1978 study reported an interesting experiment in which children were asked to color in a shape while looking at happy and sad pictures. While looking at the happy scenes they chose orange, yellow, green and blue, but used brown, black and red when looking at sad scenes.[2] Once you are able to see the colors clearly in people's auras you will be able to tell their emotional states simply by looking at the quality of the colors.

Incidentally, children are often very good at seeing auras. Elaine Murray, in her book *A Layman's Guide to New Age and Spiritual Terms*, tells of her experiences in working with eleven and twelve-year-old children while teaching in Ontario. Although she could not see auras herself at the time, she discovered that about seventy-five percent of her students were able to see auras, complete with colors.[3]

We use colors all the time to express our emotions. "I saw red," we might say when we are angry. "I'm feeling blue." "I'm green with envy." "I'm in the pink today." "He's in a black mood." These common sayings must have begun after people saw emotions revealed this way in people's auras.

In 1932, Robert Gerard, an American scientist, conducted a series of experiments with prisoners. He discovered that exposure to red light excited them and made them more aggressive. However, a blue light calmed them down. More recently, Alexander Schauss discovered that aggressiveness in prisoners decreased when they were exposed to pink light. He found that pink jail cells appeared to tranquilize their occupants and make it impossible for them to become angry. The U.S. Navy immediately started painting its detention rooms pink, and today hundreds of institutions across the country place angry inmates in pink cells to calm them down.[4]

Another experiment was conducted by Jack Widgerey, a color coordinator, when he was asked to decorate two police interviewing rooms. One was painted in soft greens and beiges, and the other in bright red and green.

The police used the first room to interview victims of crimes and their families, and the second one to interview suspects. They discovered that suspects spoke much more in the second room, making it much easier to obtain statements.

We respond to color all the time, whether we are aware of it or not. Fast food chains, for instance, know that orange stimulates the appetite and red makes time seem to pass more quickly. Consequently, when the two colors are combined, customers will buy more and eat it quickly, making room for more customers.

Once you have learned how to see the misty surround that forms the aura it is just a matter of time before you start seeing colors. For some people this may be measured in minutes, but most people need days or weeks before the colors start to appear. It is important not to become impatient. I found in my classes that the people who failed to see the colors quickly usually became very frustrated, and this impeded their progress. Allow whatever time it takes. Just be confident that the colors will appear when the time is right.

The colors usually start as a faint coloration. Most people sense the aura becoming gray and then blue as they develop their color awareness. This blue is probably the health aura that began forming when we were born.

Gradually, other colors will start to reveal themselves. They start by appearing almost washed out, as if the colors had been there, but have almost faded away. Some people spend a period of time wondering if they are really seeing colors, or if their imaginations are playing tricks on them.

In time, one color will tend to dominate the aura, and it will gradually grow in both size and intensity. This is known as the ground color. This color is extremely important as it reveals what the person should be doing with his or her life. It doesn't necessarily reveal if the person is doing the right thing, though naturally, someone who is completely fulfilled will have a glorious, vibrant aura in contrast to someone who has no idea where he or she is going.

With practice, the quality of this color will tell you a great deal about the person you are looking at. Ideally, the ground color should be large in size, rich in intensity and almost luminous in appearance. Someone who is dishonest will experience a shrinking in the size of the aura and the colors tend to become murky.

Some years ago I did a series of lectures for the inmates in a prison. It was fascinating to see that many of them had decidedly murky auras, but a handful had strikingly beautiful auras. These people were all sitting together, and I discovered later that they were the ones who were intent on rehabilitating themselves. The guards were surprised that I was able to point out this group as being different from the others, and assumed that I had realized this from the questions they had been asking.

Most people, of course, have auras that are neither rich nor murky. These are the people who get through life as best they can, without extending themselves too much. The more you look at auras, the more you will realize how much potential we all waste. Fortunately, some people realize at some stage in their lives that they are capable of doing much more than they have been, and become motivated and transform their lives. When this happens it is reflected strongly in the aura.

Every color has a meaning that can be interpreted.

Meanings of the Ground Colors

The basic colors follow the rainbow, and you will soon see that we all have each of the rainbow colors inside our auras. However, the aura can also contain colors that are not present in the rainbow.

Red
Potential: *Leadership*

This is a powerful color to have. It gives the person a strong ego and a desire to achieve and become successful. This color is often very subdued in childhood, particularly if the person is forced to fit in with the family's desires. Consequently, the aura can sometimes appear squashed and dull. Once the person reaches adulthood and is able to stand on his or her own two feet, the aura expands, showing that the person is now capable of doing whatever it is he or she should be doing.

People with a red ground color frequently achieve positions of responsibility and leadership as they have the necessary drive, energy and charisma to inspire others. They are also affectionate and warm-hearted. Red can also denote physical courage.

The negative traits of red are nervousness and self-centeredness.

Orange
Potential: *Harmony and cooperation*

Orange is a warm, caring color and you will find this as the ground color in people who are naturally intuitive, tactful and easy to get along with. They are able to make people feel at ease, and often find themselves in positions where they have to smooth "troubled waters." They are thoughtful, down to earth, capable, practical people who keep their feet firmly planted on the ground.

The negative traits of orange are laziness and a "couldn't care less" attitude.

Yellow
Potential: *Creativity, mental brilliance*

People with a yellow ground color are enthusiastic, excitable and changeable. They are quick thinkers and enjoy entertaining and being entertained by others. They are gregarious, sociable and enjoy lengthy conversations on almost any topic. They are keen to learn, but often dabble and skim over the surface of many subjects, rather than take one subject as far as they can.

The negative traits of yellow are timidity and a tendency to lie.

Green
Potential: *Healing*

Green is a peaceful color and people who have this as their ground color are peace-loving and make natural healers. They are cooperative, trustworthy and generous. They may appear placid and easy-going, but can also be highly obstinate and stubborn when they feel it necessary. The only way to change the minds of people with a green ground color is to make them think that the idea is their own.

Rigidity and fixity of outlook are the negative traits of green.

Blue
Potential: *Variety*

Blue is a wonderful color to have as the ground color as these people are naturally positive and enthusiastic. Consequently, their auras are normally large and vibrant. They have as many ups and downs as everyone else, but somehow always manage to climb out of the troughs with apparent ease. People with a blue ground color always remain young at heart. They are sincere, honest and usually say exactly what is on their mind.

The negative trait of blue is difficulty in finishing tasks. They are usually better at starting things, often with great enthusiasm, than they are at completing them.

Indigo
Potential: *Responsibility for others*

It is often difficult to determine this color as the ground color, as it can sometimes appear to be almost purple. As it is a warm, healing and nurturing color, people with it as their ground color usually end up in some humanitarian type occupation. They enjoy helping and supporting others, and find their greatest happiness when surrounded by the people they love.

The negative trait of indigo is an inability to say "no." These people can be taken advantage of by others very easily.

Violet
Potential: *Spiritual and intellectual progress*

It is no coincidence that bishops wear purple robes. People with violet as their ground color develop spiritually all the way through their lives. The degree to which they have developed so far can be determined by the quality of this color in their auras. Many people with a violet ground color try to deny this side of their nature. This does not bring happiness, and they will be aware that they are not doing what they should with their lives. Once they start to learn and grow in knowledge and wisdom, their auras also start to grow and become more vibrant.

The negative trait of violet is an air of superiority that can be off-putting to others.

Silver
Potential: *Idealism*

It is unusual to find silver as the ground color, though it is frequently seen as one of the other colors in auras. People who have it as their ground color are full of great ideas, yet sadly, most of them are impractical. These people often lack motivation and become dreamers, rather than doers. Once they become motivated and find an idea that is worth pursuing, their progress can be a joy to behold.

Gold
Potential: *Unlimited*

This is the most powerful color of all to have as a ground color. It gives people with it the ability to handle large-scale projects and to achieve virtually anything they set their minds on. They are charismatic, hard working, patient, goal-setting people. They usually achieve their greatest successes late in life. It is not surprising that the paintings of halos around saints and other spiritual people are usually gold, denoting their unlimited potential.

Pink
Potential: *Financial and material success*

This delicate-looking color frequently appears as the ground color of determined, stubborn people. They set their sights high and then go after their goals with unwavering determination. It is not surprising that they are often found in positions of power and responsibility. However, deep down, they are modest and unassuming people who enjoy a quiet life. They are also loving, gentle and kind, and are usually happiest when surrounded by their loved ones.

Bronze
Potential: *Humanitarianism*

This color usually appears as an autumn tint, and its almost rusty appearance can be strikingly attractive. People who have bronze as their ground color are caring, concerned, philanthropic humanitarians. They are soft-hearted and generous. Consequently, they usually need to learn how to say "no" as they are frequently imposed on by others.

White
Potential: *Illumination and inspiration*

White is the color of purity and is seldom seen as the ground color. As all the colors come from white, white is basically another name for light. People with it are self-effacing, modest, saintly humanitarians. They frequently seem to be totally lacking in ego and appear much more concerned with the well-being of other people than with their own. These people are often highly intuitive and wise beyond their years.

Once you have become used to seeing the ground color, you will gradually become aware of other colors that seem to radiate outwards through the ground color like colored streamers. These colors indicate what the person enjoys doing. Usually, one or two colors will predominate, but a few people have a veritable rainbow of colors radiating out through the ground color.

The happiest people are those whose colors combine. Some combinations may sound unlikely, but in practice work very well. For instance, someone who has a ground color of red (independence and leadership) may have flashes of orange (tact, diplomacy, gentleness) radiating through his aura. He will still have leadership qualities, but they will be expressed in a gentle manner. He will not get results by ordering people around, but would be very successful at getting people to cooperate with him.

Again, someone with a red ground color with white rays through it could become a leader in some humanitarian pursuit. This person would experience difficulties, though, if she tried to use her leadership talents solely in the business arena. To be happy and fulfilled she would need to balance the two energies, even though they may appear to oppose each other. This person is likely to start out in life by using the red and ignoring the white. At some stage, she will realize that she is fighting against herself, and hopefully will reassess her life and move on to her true path.

This is where the ability to see and read auras can be extremely practical. Someone who can see the red and white in this person's aura would be able to advise her of the path she should be on. It is likely that deep inside she would be aware of what she should be doing, but would probably be fighting it every step of the way. However, her progress, fulfillment and personal happiness will increase enormously once she is working in harmony with her aura colors.

Radiating Colors

Red
People with red radiating through their auras like to be in charge. They love responsibility and enjoy making decisions. They seek power and the financial rewards that can come from it.

Orange
People with orange radiating through their auras enjoy spending time with close friends and family. They are naturally intuitive, nurturing and caring.

Yellow
People with yellow radiating through their auras enjoy new ideas. They like expressing themselves in various ways, such as singing, dancing, writing, painting, and—especially—talking.

Green

People with green radiating through their auras enjoy challenges and opportunities to prove themselves. They are willing to work tirelessly for however long it takes to achieve their goals. They make natural healers.

Blue

People with blue radiating through their auras enjoy freedom and variety. They hate being limited or restricted in any way. The most unsuitable occupation for them would be a standard nine-to-five job. They enjoy travel and seeing new places and faces.

Indigo

People with indigo radiating through their auras enjoy helping others, particularly people they care about. They enjoy solving family problems and are usually the first person family members confide in when there is a problem.

Violet

People with violet radiating through their auras enjoy time on their own to learn and grow in knowledge and wisdom. They frequently become involved in spiritual or metaphysical activities, as they like to learn the hidden truths behind all things.

Silver

People with silver radiating through their auras enjoy coming up with great ideas. It makes no difference to them whether these ideas are practical: it is the ideas themselves that are important. They can become totally lost inside their imaginations, and are happiest in this world of their own where everything is perfect.

Gold
People with gold radiating through their auras enjoy large-scale undertakings. They seek challenges that can stretch them and take them out of their comfort zones.

Pink
People with pink radiating through their auras enjoy planning and dreaming about financial success. If they learn to harmonize the pink with their ground color they can become astonishingly successful.

White
People with white radiating through their auras are idealistic, peace-loving people. They enjoy supporting causes that they believe in, and seek a better world for future generations.

The aura consists of several layers, known as subtle bodies, and sometimes the colors of these vary. In practice, most clairvoyants see the aura as the etheric plane, surrounded by a single layer, with different colors inside it. However, as you become more and more aware of auras, you may well start seeing different layers making up the aura. There are seven of these:

1. The Physical Etheric Plane
2. The Astral Plane
3. The Lower Mental Plane

4. The Higher Mental Plane
5. The Spiritual Plane
6. The Intuitional Plane
7. The Absolute Plane

These are all connected with the chakras, which we will discuss in the next chapter.

Hints If You Are Having Difficulty

Some people have no problems seeing colors inside the aura. However, others find it painfully difficult. Years ago, a woman in one of my classes was able to see the almost invisible misty surround immediately. However, no matter how much she practiced, she was not able to see any colors. She found it very frustrating when other people in the class who had found it hard to see the first signs of the aura went on to see the colors with apparent ease.

Fortunately, I was able to help this woman by teaching her how to dowse for the colors. Once she knew what colors she was looking for, she found that her color awareness grew almost overnight. In retrospect, her biggest problem was anxiety. Because she was the first person in the class to see auras, she expected to be the first to see the aura colors as well. She became frustrated when everyone else in the class could see colors, and this frustration made her try too hard.

As mentioned before, it is important to simply relax and allow the colors to gradually appear. Everyone is different. Some people see colors from the very start. Others spend weeks or months developing this skill.

It is helpful if you become more aware of, and in tune with, different colors. Become aware of the colors you wear, and ask yourself why you are wearing those particular colors. Experiment by wearing different colors and seeing how you feel while wearing them. You will find your awareness of color growing enormously, making it much easier for you to see auras.

Some years ago a friend of mine had to give a speech to a group of colleagues and felt inadequate to the task. She worried constantly about it, and finally I suggested that she wear some red to give her confidence. I meant a blouse, perhaps, but she bought herself a red suit and red shoes, and gave a dynamic presentation. This experience increased her color awareness, and she is now happy to wear bright colors. In the past, most of her clothing was gray or fawn.

Become aware of the colors that other people wear. Ask yourself what benefit, if any, these people are gaining from the colors they have chosen.

While you are falling asleep in bed at night, visualize pleasant scenes in your mind and see them as clearly as you can. For instance, you might see yourself at a favorite beach. See and feel the texture of the sand beneath your feet. Smell the salty air, and look at—and see as clearly as you can—the colors of the sand, sea and sky.

Some years ago I spent a few pleasant days staying in a log cabin high up in the woods. If I want to visualize a pleasant scene, I picture the view from the front door of this cabin, gazing over miles and miles of pine forests at the snow-covered peaks of the mountains beyond. I can easily recall how peaceful, tranquil and relaxing it was. I can also smell the scent of pine and feel the cool breeze. Most of all, though, I recapture and see again the gorgeous colors that surrounded me.

Many of my students have found doodling with colored markers a helpful exercise in developing color awareness. I tell them to draw a picture or design without paying much attention to the colors they are using. Afterwards, they look at the colors and recapture how they felt while they were drawing. If they felt sad, lonely or depressed they would invariably choose blacks and browns, but if they felt happy and on top of the world, they would use a rainbow of bright, cheerful colors.

Drawing like this is an excellent way to release unwanted, negative feelings. It is also extremely useful in developing aura awareness as it involves using the right-hand side of the brain, which is necessary to see auras.

Finally, breathing in the colors can be very helpful. To do this, you simply need to close your eyes and visualize yourself inhaling a big breath of red air. As you exhale, visualize this red air spreading throughout your entire body. Do this three or four times with the color red, and then repeat it with orange. Gradually work your way through the entire rainbow. Notice how you feel as you breathe in the different colors. This exercise can be very useful in learning the meanings of each color, as you actually experience the effects of each one in your own body.

Dowsing for the Colors

To do this all you need are the angle rods that you used for sensing for the outer edge of the aura. It is helpful if the person whose aura you are trying to see is present, but it is not essential.

Start by holding the angle rods so that the long sections are placed directly forward. Ask the rods to give you a positive response. I find it helpful to ask this out loud.

"What movement represents 'yes'?" I ask.

In my case, the angle rods move inward until they are overlapping each other. You may find that they move outward. A friend of mine knows the answer is positive when the angle rods move toward each other but stop at a ninety-degree angle. It makes no difference what movements the angle rods make, just as long as you know it indicates a positive response.

Suppose you are dowsing the colors of a man named Bill. You start by holding the angle rods in front of you and ask, "Is the ground color in Bill's aura red?"

If there is no response to this, ask, "Is the ground color in Bill's aura orange?"

Continue going through the colors until you get a positive reaction. I carry on through all the colors, even if I receive a positive reaction to the first one I ask about. This is purely to confirm that I have the correct answer.

Once you have the ground color, you can ask your angle rods to tell you what the radiating colors are. Remember, with radiating colors you may receive more than one positive response.

Suppose we discover that Bill has a blue ground color, with red and violet radiating colors. We now know what colors we are looking for, and this makes discerning them that much easier.

In practice, most people need do this only a few times. After this their color awareness will have developed sufficiently for them to see the full aura without the help of their angle rods.

Determining the Colors with Numerology

Another method of finding people's aura colors is to use numerology. Every number in numerology relates to a specific color:[5]

1	Red
2	Orange
3	Yellow
4	Green
5	Blue
6	Indigo
7	Violet
8	Pink
9	Bronze
11	Silver
22	Gold

The ground color is determined from the person's Life Path number. This is the most important number in Pythagorean numerology as it represents the person's purpose in life. You will remember that the ground color reveals what the person should be doing with his or her life. This is why the person's ground color and the color relating to his or her Life Path are usually—but not always—the same.

The Life Path is determined by making a sum of the person's full date of birth. Let's assume we are determining the color of someone born on April 28, 1980. We make a sum of these numbers:

$$
\begin{array}{ll}
4 & \text{(month)} \\
28 & \text{(day)} \\
\underline{1980} & \text{(year)} \\
2012 &
\end{array}
$$

The total (2012) is then reduced down to a single digit by adding them together: $2 + 0 + 1 + 2 = 5$.

This person's Life Path number is 5, and as 5 relates to the color blue, he or she is likely to have a blue ground color in his or her aura.

Here is another example. This time of a young woman born on March 12, 1975:

$$
\begin{array}{ll}
3 & \text{(month)} \\
12 & \text{(day)} \\
\underline{1975} & \text{(year)} \\
1990 &
\end{array}
$$

We then reduce the total to a single digit: $1 + 9 + 9 + 0 = 19$, and $1 + 9 = 10$, and finally $1 + 0 = 1$. This young woman has a Life Path number of 1, which means her ground color is probably red.

There are just two exceptions to reducing the total down to a single digit. This is when you find either an 11 or a 22 during the reducing process. These numbers are known as Master Numbers in numerology and are not reduced down to a 2 or a 4. This is because the people who have them are blessed with greater potential than the rest of us.[6]

We also create a sum in the way I have described to avoid losing any master numbers. I have a good friend who was born on February 29, 1944. When we work out her Life Path number using the method just described we find that she is a 22:

$$2 \text{ (month)}$$
$$29 \text{ (day)}$$
$$\underline{1944} \text{ (year)}$$
$$1975 \text{ and } 1 + 9 + 7 + 5 = 22$$

If we added up her numbers in a straight line we would lose the master number: 2 (month) + 2 + 9 (day) + 1 + 9 + 4 + 4 (year) = 31, and 3 + 1 = 4.

This is why it is important to add up the month, day and year of birth by creating a sum, rather than by simply adding up all the numbers and then bringing them down to a single digit.

You will notice that we have a choice of just eleven different colors in numerology. This is why this method is not 100% perfect. Usually, the two colors will be the same, but it is possible that they may differ.

Someone may have a Life Path of 7, which relates to the color violet, but may have a white aura. In fact, he or she may have any other color at all as the ground color. This is because the Life Path number represents the person's purpose in life.

Consequently, the color indicated by the Life Path will certainly appear somewhere in the aura, but may not be the ground color, as that reveals what the person should be doing with his or her life. In practice, the colors will be compatible, when they are not the same.

The Life Path number is perhaps 95% accurate in determining a person's ground color. Fortunately, the other main numbers in numerology are extremely accurate in determining the radiating colors.

These numbers come from the name the person is usually known by. This can become complicated as people can be known by a variety of names. Bill Smith might be known to his parents as William. His friends may call him Bill, but at work he is known as W.J., as his middle name is James. At the bank he is known as William James Smith. However, he signs his checks W. J. Smith. As a child he was known as Billy-boy. His wife usually calls him "Teddy Bear." To make it even harder, he was adopted at the age of three months. When he was born he was given the name William James Callaghan, but took on the name Smith when he was adopted. Which name do we use?

In practice, we use the name he is most comfortable with. This is usually the name his friends know him by. So in this case, we would use the name Bill Smith.

This is in contrast to traditional numerology, where we use the person's full name at birth.

We turn the letters of Bill's name into numbers using the following chart:

1	2	3	4	5	6	7	8	9
A	B	C	D	E	F	G	H	I
J	K	L	M	N	O	P	Q	R
S	T	U	V	W	X	Y	Z	

With the name Bill Smith we find the following total:
BILL SMITH
2933 14928, and 2 + 9 + 3 + 3 (Bill) + 1 + 4 + 9 + 2
+ 8 (Smith) = 41, and 4 + 1 = 5.

The number 5 is Bill's Expression number in numerology and represents his natural abilities. Bill is obviously a versatile person.

We know that 5 relates to the color blue, so Bill will have this color radiating outwards through his ground color.

The next most important number in numerology is the Soul's Urge. This number is created by adding up the value of all the vowels in the person's name. Bill has just two vowels (an "I" in both his first and last names).

We add the numbers relating to the letter "I" together: 9 + 9 = 18, and 1 + 8 = 9. Bill's Soul Urge number is 9, which relates to bronze. Bill will also have autumn tints radiating outwards in his aura.

Unfortunately, there is also one exception to the rules in determining the Soul's Urge. The letter "Y" is usually classed as a vowel, as normally it acts as a vowel (as in the name "Lynda") or is not pronounced (as in "Kay"). However, if it is pronounced (as in "Yolande"), it is classed as a consonant.

Gaining Color Awareness

There are two useful exercises to help you gain color awareness. The first one is as part of a relaxation exercise and several people I know use it in bed at night to help them fall asleep.

Rainbow Meditation

Sit down in a comfortable chair or lie down in bed and close your eyes. Take several deep breaths, concentrating on your breathing. As you exhale say to yourself "I'm calm and relaxed." When you are feeling totally relaxed imagine a beautiful, perfect rainbow in your mind. Picture it as clearly as you can.

In your imagination, walk up to it and step inside the red. Visualize yourself completely surrounded and bathed by the color red. Feel it permeating into your body and revitalizing every cell and organ. It may feel as if the red is a flowing river of energy, reaching out to enfold you as it passes through and around you.

When you feel completely suffused with red, move further into the rainbow and enter the orange. Feel the peace and contentment that flows into you as you imagine yourself completely surrounded by orange energy.

Carry on into the beautiful, stimulating yellow. Although you will find it mentally stimulating, it will also have a calming effect on your nerves and body.

After you have been completely bathed in the yellow energy, move on into the green. Notice how calming and soothing it is. All the stress and strain will simply fall away as you are enfolded and refreshed by this healing energy.

Step out of the green into the blue. You will notice that you are surrounded briefly by turquoise as you move deeper into the visionary blue. You will feel a strong desire to move forward and make something of your life as you allow yourself to be bathed by the brilliant blue. You will feel healthier and more enthusiastic than you have been for a long, long time.

It is just a single step to move into the indigo, a deep, intense, illuminating color. Feel its healing, soothing, comforting energy. It is so beneficial to spend time bathed and washed in blue and indigo.

Finally, move on into the violet band and feel the rapid increase in your awareness and understanding of life. Feel your mind opening up to intuition and inspiration.

Once you have finished this exercise, pause and relax quietly for a few moments before opening your eyes. You will feel fresh and totally revitalized. However, the greatest advantage of doing this exercise for our purposes is because of the increased color awareness it gives. As you imagine yourself surrounded and bathed by each color you will gain insights into the meanings and relationships of each color. You will be gaining all the advantages of a meditation, plus increased insight into the colors of the rainbow.

Single Color Auras

Another excellent way of gaining color awareness is to see the auras surrounding individual colors. This is because single color auras appear to be considerably easier to see than the human aura. For my psychic development classes I cover children's play blocks with sheets of colored cellophane. Each block is covered with a different color of cellophane.

I place the blocks one at a time on a tabletop and allow the class to look at them. I start with the blue block, followed by the red, as these seem to be the easiest colors around which to see auras. It is best if my pupils are sitting at least three feet away from the block. I suggest that they look slightly to one side of the block and focus on the wall behind it. As they stare at the wall I tell them to remain relaxed. Usually, it is only a matter of seconds before everyone notices a surround of a different color to the one they are looking at. They see a yellow aura around the blue block and a green aura around the red one. These are known as complementary colors.

Once they have seen these I quickly replace them with the other blocks and again everyone is able to see the auras surrounding them.

You can do this same exercise using sheets of cardboard, each printed in a different color.

The purpose of this exercise was to show the class that auras exist around everything, and all they needed to do was relax and remain aware for them to become visible. However, it is also a perfect exercise for people who are having difficulty in seeing the colors inside auras.

In practice, you will find both dowsing and numerology useful aids when you first start. However, as your awareness of the aura colors increases, you will find that you will need these less and less.

Do not become reliant on these artificial aids. They can be very useful in telling you which colors to look for, but if you simply work the colors out using these, you will slow down your progress. Keep on working at seeing the colors. Be patient and allow it to happen.

So far there has not been much scientific research into the colors of the aura and their meanings. However, what research has been done indicates that the colors in the aura "are significant indicators of personal traits."[7]

The Chakras

5

The chakras are seven centers of power located alongside the spinal column in the etheric body (Figure 5.1). In Hindu yoga it is believed that *prana*, the life force, flows around our bodies through a network of tiny channels called *nadis*. There are said to be 72,000 nadis inside the human subtle body.[1] The chakras are situated on the principal nadi (the *sushumna*) which runs alongside the spinal column. They are revolving, wheel-like circles of subtle energies that absorb higher energies and transform them into a useable form that can be utilized in the body. In the East they are often depicted as lotus flowers, a circle surrounded by petals.

Our bodies contain currents of both positive and negative energies that come directly from our breath. The right side of the body contains positive energy, and

the left side negative.
These energies influ-
ence the directions the
chakras revolve in.
Each chakra appears to
revolve in the opposite
direction to the chakras
above and below it.

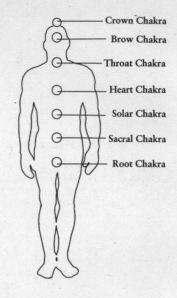

You will have felt
the enormous energy
emanating from these
chakras when you were
feeling the aura, so will
have a good idea of
how powerful they are.

Each chakra has a
name and a color that

Figure 5.1. The seven chakra centers

spirals outwards from its center. Each chakra relates
to a color of the rainbow. Consequently, our auras
contain at least a small portion of every color of the
rainbow.

Chakras have been known and utilized in the East for
thousands of years, but until recently have been ignored
by Western scientists. In the 1970s, Dr. Hiroshi
Motoyama of Japan conducted research to prove or dis-
prove the existence of chakras. His results were positive
and are reported in his book *Science and the Evolution
of Consciousness: Chakras, Ki, and Psi.*[2] Dr. Motoyama
conducted tests inside a specially designed lead-lined
booth to see if he could measure the bioenergetic/bio-
electrical output from the chakras. A moveable copper

electrode was placed close to the chakra that was being tested to measure the bioelectrical field. When tests were done on people who claimed that they had opened out or awakened specific chakras, Dr. Motoyama found that the amplitude and frequency of the electrical field around the chakra was significantly greater than it was around the same chakra in his test subjects.

Dr. Motoyama also discovered that certain people could consciously project energy through their chakras to create electrical field disturbances. Unlike many psychic experiments, this one is repeatable and has been demonstrated many times in university laboratories .[3]

Another interesting experiment was performed by Dr. Valerie Hunt at UCLA. She was conducting experiments to determine the therapeutic effects of a manipulative technique known as Rolfing and was using EMG electrodes, which are normally used to measure the electrical potential of muscles. She found that the readings she obtained over the chakra positions were far higher than in other parts of the body.[4]

A further astounding discovery of this series of experiments involved Rosalyn Bruyere, a gifted psychic. While Dr. Hunt monitored the chakras electronically, Rosalyn Bruyere observed the changes in the volunteers' auras. Dr. Hunt found that the psychic's comments about the color changes inside the aura correlated perfectly with the EMG electrode recordings. They found that every time Bruyere mentioned seeing, for instance, red in the aura, a distinctive wave pattern would be registering on the recording equipment. The same thing applied to every other color.[5]

The Quatern

The four bottom chakras are often represented as a square, known as the quatern. They have a slower vibration than the three topmost chakras and are solidly grounded in the earth. Each of these chakras is related to one of the traditional elements of fire, earth, air and water.

Root Chakra
(Muladhara)

Color: *Red*
Element: *Earth*
Sense: *Smell*
Desires: *Physical contact*
Challenge: *To think before acting*
Keyword: *Physical*

The root chakra is situated at the base of the spine and gives us the feeling of security and comfort. The Sanskrit word *muladhara* means "support." In effect, the root chakra builds up vitality and keeps us firmly grounded to the earth. It makes us feel vibrant, alive and full of energy. At an emotional level it gives courage and persistence. The root chakra also governs our sense of smell and the solid parts of our bodies, such as teeth, bones, and nails. It pays a major role in our survival as it also controls our fight-or-flight responses. When this chakra is under-stimulated we feel nervous and insecure. Consequently, fear can gather inside this chakra. When it is over-stimulated we can be domineering, self-centered, and addicted to money and sex.

Sacral Chakra
(Svadisthana)

Color: *Orange*
Element: *Water*
Sense: *Taste*
Desires: *Respect and acceptance*
Challenge: *To love and serve others*
Keyword: *Social*

The sacral chakra is situated at the level of the sacrum in the small of the back, about two inches below the navel. As this chakra relates to the element water, it is concerned with the fluidic functions of the body. It represents sexuality, creativity, and emotional balance. *Svadisthana* means "home of the vital force." This chakra stimulates optimism and hope on an emotional level. It also relates to our sense of taste. People who relate easily to others have well-balanced sacral chakras. This gives them the necessary fluidity to interact smoothly and effectively. If this chakra is not working efficiently we can experience illnesses such as arthritis. These often come from the negative emotions of anger, frustration, and resentment that are caused when this chakra is under-stimulated. When the sacral chakra is over-stimulated we are manipulative, aggressive and overly self-indulgent.

Solar Chakra
(Manipuraka)

Color: *Yellow*
Element: *Fire*
Sense: *Sight*
Desires: To *understand*
Challenge: To *communicate effectively with loved ones*
Keyword: *Intellect*

The solar, or solar plexus, chakra is situated at the level of the solar plexus. The word *manipuraka* means "jewel of the navel." It gives us warmth, good self-esteem and happiness. This chakra is concerned with two areas. When working efficiently, it relates to absorption and assimilation of food, giving good digestion and a feeling of physical well-being. It also relates to our eyes. This is not surprising when you consider how much brighter everything seems to be when we are feeling happy and content. This chakra also relates to sensitivity. On an emotional level this chakra creates optimism, creativity, self-respect, and confidence. Anger and hostility can build up inside the solar chakra when the person is living negatively.

When this chakra is over-stimulated we become workaholics, perfectionists, and overly demanding. When under-stimulated, we lack confidence, become confused and feel that we have no control over our lives.

Heart Chakra
(Anahatha)

Color:	*Green*
Element:	*Air*
Sense:	*Touch*
Desires:	*To love and be loved*
Challenge:	*To gain confidence*
Keyword:	*Emotions*

The heart chakra is situated in the center of the chest, in line with the heart. It relates to love, harmony, sympathetic understanding and the sense of touch. When we are "in touch" with someone our heart (emotions) goes out to them. In the Far East this chakra of love is often referred to as the "house of the soul." *Anahatha* means "unbeaten." On the emotional level this chakra enhances compassion, self-acceptance and respect for self and others. These people are in touch with their feelings and nurture themselves and others.

You are bound to know people who have an under-stimulated heart chakra. They are inclined to be over-sensitive, overly sympathetic, and have a need to constantly give to others. They feel sorry for themselves and are constantly afraid. Most co-dependents have under-stimulated heart chakras. If this chakra is over-stimulated we become possessive, demanding, moody, and controlling.

The Trinity

The three top chakras are known as the trinity or triad. They are vibrating at a higher level than the lower four chakras. The three chakras of the trinity relate to the quadruplicities of astrology known as cardinal, fixed, and mutable. The cardinal signs (Aries, Cancer, Libra, and Capricorn) are outgoing, energetic, and expressive. The fixed signs (Taurus, Leo, Scorpio, and Aquarius) are rigid, stubborn, and tenacious. The mutable signs (Gemini, Virgo, Sagittarius, and Pisces) are adaptable and able to adjust to changing circumstances.

Throat Chakra
(Visshudha)

Color: *Blue*
Quadruplicity: *Fixed*
Sense: *Sound*
Desires: *Inner peace*
Challenge: *To risk*
Keyword: *Concepts*

The throat chakra is situated at the level of the throat. *Visshudha* means "pure." The throat chakra is a vital element in transmitting thought and ideas from the brow chakra to the four lower chakras. It relates to sound, especially the voice. It is the chakra of communication and self-expression. At an emotional level it enhances idealism, love, and understanding. When properly balanced this chakra gives contentment, peace of mind, a good sense of timing, and a strong faith. When it is over-stimulated we can become arrogant, dogmatic, sarcastic, and overbearing. When it is under-stimulated we become weak, devious, and unreliable.

Brow Chakra
(Ajna)

Color: *Indigo*
Quadruplicity: *Mutable*
Desires: *To be in harmony with the Universe*
Challenge: *To make one's dreams a reality*
Keyword: *Intuition*

The brow chakra is situated in the forehead, between the eyebrows. In Sanskrit, this chakra is called *Ajna*, which means "command." This chakra governs the mind and is the command center that controls all the other chakras. Nothing is ever created without someone thinking it first. This is the function of the brow chakra. Unfortunately, most of us have little or no control over our thought patterns. At an emotional level it increases our understanding of the everyday world by making us aware of our spiritual natures.

All intuition comes from the brow chakra, even such minor examples as picking up other people's moods and feelings. Have you ever spent time with someone full of negative energy, and left feeling totally drained? You have been influenced by this person's negative energy, even though he or she may not have expressed anything but positive or neutral ideas out loud. We are all influenced on a subliminal level by others.

When this chakra is over-stimulated we become proud, authoritative, manipulative, and dogmatic. Adolf Hitler must have had an over-stimulated brow chakra. When this chakra is under-stimulated we become non-assertive, timid failures.

Crown Chakra
(Sahasrara)

Color: *Violet*
Quadruplicity: *Cardinal*
Desires: *Universal understanding*
Challenge: *To grow in knowledge and wisdom*
Keyword: *Spirituality*

The crown chakra is situated at the very top of the head and controls the strongest energy vibrations in the body. The crown chakra is often depicted as a halo by artists when painting someone who is spiritually evolved. The tonsure of monks began as a way of exposing this area.[6] The Sanskrit word *sahasrara* means "thousand," and the symbol of the crown chakra is the thousand-petaled lotus.

The crown chakra balances and harmonizes the interior and exterior sides of our natures. It also governs the mystical, spiritual level where one realizes the interconnectedness of all living things. It is extremely difficult to leave the concept of individuality behind and become a part of the universe in this way. However, by doing so, one really becomes whole as our baser natures are forgotten and left behind, allowing us to really live.

When this chakra is over-stimulated we become frustrated, destructive and depressed. Severe migraine headaches are common when this chakra is over-stimulated. When the crown chakra is under-stimulated we become withdrawn, uncommunicative and lack any joy in life.

As you start to see the different chakras you will notice that they are not all of equal size or intensity. One person may have a large, vibrant, alive, rapidly moving throat chakra, and the next person may have a throat chakra that is small, dull, and sluggish. This means that the first person is using his or her throat chakra positively, while the second person is not making the most of his or her potential in this area.

Fortunately, if the person will give you permission to do so, you are able to rectify the lethargic throat chakra and effectively balance the person's energies. This is called aura balancing.

Aura Balancing

In Chapter Two we learned how to dowse for the aura using angle rods. We are now going to dowse using a pendulum.

A pendulum is simply a weight attached to a piece of thread, string, or fine chain. Almost anything will do, but it is easier to interpret the results if the weight is at least a few ounces.

There are a large number of commercially made pendulums available at psychic and New Age bookstores. If you decide to buy one of these, try several before making a decision. You will find that some pendulums react more easily for you than others. You can also buy aura pendulums (sometimes known as spectrum pendulums). These pendulums have all the colors of the rainbow depicted on the side. They also have a small indicator that can slide up and down to enable you to indicate the specific color you are dowsing for. Many people find these helpful; I have one that I use. How-

Figure 5.2.
Dowsing with pendulum

ever, a normal pendulum will give you the same results (Figure 5.2).

Hold the cord of the pendulum between your thumb and first finger and suspend over Figure 5.3. Ask the pendulum which direction represents "yes." Be patient, and after a while your pendulum will start to move. It may move upwards and downwards, or from side to side, or in a circular motion, either clockwise or counter-clockwise.

Once you know which way indicates "yes," hold the pendulum still for a moment over the center of the diagram and then ask it which direction represents "no." After a while the pendulum will react and give you this information."

It pays to check your pendulum's movements every now and again. Many people find that once a pendulum gives a "yes" and "no"

Figure 5.3.

response, those movements will remain the same for ever. However, some people find that they change from time to time. Consequently, it is a good idea to get into the habit of asking your pendulum which movement indicates "yes" and which way "no," every so often.

Now we can balance our friend's aura using the pendulum.

Ask your friend to lie down comfortably on his or her back. I usually provide a small pillow for them to rest their head.

If you have an aura pendulum, set the indicator so that it is indicating the red. If you are using a normal pendulum, say to yourself, "I am now checking the root chakra."

Suspend the pendulum over the base of the spine, roughly corresponding to the position of the genitals. Ask the pendulum, "Is my friend's root chakra in good health?"

If the reply is positive, nothing further need be done, and we can move on to the sacral chakra and check it. (Remember, of course, when using an aura pendulum to change the position of the indicator to orange.)

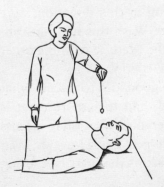

Figure 5.4.
Balancing chakra with pendulum

However, if the pendulum gives a negative response, indicating that the root chakra is not in good health, we need to check further. In practice, I check each chakra first, before going back to correct any imbalances (Figure 5.4).

Once I have checked all seven chakras, I ask my pendulum which chakra is most negative. I do this by asking my pendulum about each one in order. "Is the root chakra the most negative? Is the sacral chakra most negative?" and so on, until I have determined the answer.

At this stage we need to ask our pendulum two more questions. Suspend it over Figure 5.3 again and ask it, "Which direction indicates negative energies?" and "Which direction indicates positive energies?"

Fill a glass with water and place the fingers of the hand that is not holding the pendulum into it.

Suspend the pendulum over the chakra that is most negative and ask the pendulum to extract all the negative energies from it. The pendulum will start moving in the direction that indicates negativity. What is happening, in effect, is that the negativity is traveling up the pendulum, into your arm and across your chest and down the other arm into the water.

As soon as it stops moving in this direction, take your fingers out of the water. Wash this hand in running water, and then repeat the exercise with the other chakras that showed negative energy.

As you are doing this it is a good idea to discuss what is going on with your friend, and to inquire what is causing the negativity. Not everyone will wish to discuss this with you, and you must respect this. However, even in these cases, I mention the factors that may be causing the negativity and give suggestions that, hopefully, the person will act upon. Naturally, if you are going to do aura balancing you need to be caring, sensitive, gentle and understanding in your approach and manner.

Sometimes people do not know the causes of their negativity. This could be because they have buried their problems so deeply that they are not aware that they are still there.

Not long ago I did an aura balancing for a well-to-do businessman. He considered himself to be an extremely positive person and could not believe that he was harboring any negativity at all. However, as I continued with the aura balancing he confided that as a child he had never cried, as his father had told him that boys don't cry. This need to conceal and control his emotions was buried deeply inside his chakras. When I finished he cried for almost twenty minutes. He brushed away my concerns, saying that they were tears of happiness. When he left he looked at least fifteen years younger than when he had arrived.

Once you have removed all of the negativity, check the chakras again to ensure that the pendulum is indicating a positive response over each one. This is because sometimes not all of the negativity has been removed. The job is not over until each chakra gives a positive response.

Then, to finish off the process, set the indicator of the aura pendulum to green and swing the pendulum all over the body in the direction that indicates a positive response. If you are using a normal pendulum, imagine green, healing energies being sent out from the pendulum to revitalize and restore your friend.

Finally, ask your friend to pour the water in the glass down the sink, at the same time thanking it for taking away all the negativity.

Your friend should feel and look full of life and energy after an aura balancing. Often people say that they feel better than they have in years. I also find, as a bonus, that I feel restored and invigorated after doing an aura balancing. Many people open up their hearts and minds after an aura balancing. This occurs even with people who were reluctant to discuss the causes of the negativity while the aura balancing was in progress.

Crystals

There are crystals that relate to each of the chakras which can be worn to help achieve balance. However, you must choose and wear them with care. Crystals are quick to absorb energy. Consequently, if you are thinking negatively, the crystal will absorb that energy and reflect it back to you later on. Crystals also absorb other people's feelings. Consequently, if you spend most of your time with bad-tempered, unhappy or depressed people, your crystal will absorb those feelings and pass them on to you.

On the other hand, if you spend a great deal of time with enthusiastic, progressive, happy people, your crystal will absorb this and reflect it on to you.

It is a good idea to wear your crystal inside your clothes, next to the skin. This helps protect it from other people's negative energy. Some people prefer to keep their crystal in a small bag around their neck for the same reason. However, this is less effective than wearing it in contact with your skin.

You need to cleanse your crystals regularly, particularly if they have gathered up negativity. Rinse them for sixty seconds under cold, running water. Hold your crystal with the termination point downwards while you do this.

Not surprisingly, the crystals for each chakra are usually chosen for their color. Consequently, a red crystal is worn to help the root chakra, and an orange one assists the sacral chakra. Many people wear clear quartz crystals. The purpose of this is to help all of the chakras, as clear crystal relates to light, which creates all of the colors. Consequently, clear quartz crystals can heal the body indirectly by providing whatever colors are required.

Root Chakra

Red garnet (best worn below the waist as it can cause headaches and dizziness)

Black obsidian (for grounding)

Smoky quartz (good for psychic, emotional and physical blocks)

Sacral Chakra

Tiger's eye (gives strength, endurance and courage)

Carnelian (enhances virility and reduces tension)

Solar Chakra

Citrine (helps concentration and reduces worry)

Malachite (a green stone that releases emotional trauma and creates joy)

Heart Chakra

Green jade (gives love, warmth and wisdom)

Rose quartz (helps you to love and nurture yourself)

Green aventurine (the dreamer's stone—gives independence and great ideas)

Throat Chakra

Sodalite (aids self-expression)

Azurite (enhances spiritual awakening)

Brow Chakra

Lapis (aids spirituality—use with care as it can cause dizziness in some people)

Fluorite (restores body after emotional upsets)

Crown Chakra

Amethyst (powerful protector)

Purple fluorite (restores body and gives spiritual awareness)

Sugilite (gives sense of purpose)

Clear quartz (contains entire rainbow and helps all the chakras)

Interpreting the Colors

$\mathbf{B}$y now you are likely to be seeing a wide variety of colors inside people's auras. It is fascinating to look at the many colors visible in everyone's aura, but this ability is not very useful unless you know what the colors mean. Every color in the aura has a meaning that can be interpreted.

The most obvious color is the ground color as this is the dominant color in the aura. Frequently, people have told me how unhappy they were with their ground color. Perhaps they imagined themselves as possessing a beautiful, spiritual violet aura, and were disappointed to learn it was an earthy, red ground color. These people are being concerned unnecessarily. They are using the traditional meanings of the colors and ignoring all the other aspects that are involved.

The traditional meanings are:

RED:	Sensuality, vitality, aggression
ORANGE:	Emotion, health
YELLOW:	Creativity, intellect
GREEN:	Healing, love of nature
BLUE:	Teacher, traveler, seeker of wisdom
INDIGO:	Caring, nurturing, humanitarian
VIOLET:	Spirituality, intuition, teacher, clairvoyant
PINK:	Materialism, goal-setting, hard work
BRONZE:	Humanitarian, self-sacrificing
WHITE:	Spirituality, purity, selflessness
SILVER:	Intuitive, idealistic, dreamer, visionary
GOLD:	Unlimited potential

I have met people with every one of these colors as their ground color. Many times they are living up to the traditional interpretations of their color. However, it is just as likely that they are doing almost the complete opposite.

For example, you will find business people with every single possible ground color. The same applies for teachers, doctors, lawyers, plumbers, clerks, and every other occupation you could possibly name. Also, among the unemployed there will be a representation of every color. Even in prisons you will find every possible ground color.

Why is this? You would expect everyone with a gold ground color to be doing something really worthwhile with his or her life. You would expect someone with a violet or white ground color to be spiritually evolved.

The fact is that people are such complex, complicated beings that it is impossible to classify them in such a simplistic way.

If you ask people with an orange ground color if they have strong emotions you will receive a mixture of replies. For some the answer will be strongly affirmative, but others will deny that emotions play any part in their life at all. No matter what the reply is, you will know that at some stage in the person's life the potential will be there to make positive use of his or her emotions.

It used to worry me to think about the number of people with silver and gold ground colors who were doing absolutely nothing with their lives. Surely, I thought, they should be so much more successful than the rest of us. However, the saying that you cannot really know anyone until you have walked a mile in his or her moccasins applies. Frequently, these people are given incredible opportunities but fail to seize them for any number of reasons.

Fear is the most common one. Fear of failing. Fear of succeeding. For many of these people it is easier to let the opportunities pass by and lead a life of mediocrity. They will be painfully aware that they are not doing what they could—or should—be doing, but fear holds them back.

The ground color simply shows what the person should be doing with his or her life. The person may be doing something completely different, and there could be any number of reasons for this.

For a while I sold printing machines. It would be hard to find anyone less mechanical than me, but I was successful at the job because I enjoyed selling. Whenever a potential purchaser asked me technical questions I had to go away and find the answer, because my brain doesn't work along practical lines. My ground color is blue. Anyone looking at my aura at the time I was calling on printing companies would have wondered why I was doing the job. I was aware that I was not doing what I should be doing, but I had a young family and a large mortgage, and the job paid extremely well. I was doing it as a means to an end.

I was fortunate in that I sold printing machines for just a short while, but many people spend their entire lives doing jobs that they are not suited for and often dislike intensely.

Needless to say, this is reflected in their auras. The colors tend to look faded and the entire aura looks tired and small. These people are living just half a life.

Contrast this with someone who is pursuing a career that he or she loves. Every morning is the start of a new day full of excitement and joy. Assume that this person also has a happy, fulfilling home life, and loves and is loved in return. This person's aura will be large and the colors will be vibrant and full of energy and life.

You may know two people with the same ground color, but one is leading a fulfilling life while the other is simply going through the motions. A stranger looking at their auras would instantly know who was fulfilled and who wasn't.

Mood Auras

Our ground colors remain throughout life, but they can be replaced temporarily by other colors as our moods change.

Suppose you are enjoying a pleasant day at work. Halfway through the day someone walks into your office and unjustly accuses you of something you haven't done. This person then storms out of your office without giving you a chance to reply. Would your emotions be affected? It is likely that your ground color would suddenly be suffused with orange to reflect your heightened emotional state.

As you brood about this unjust accusation you might become angry. The orange would fade and become intermingled with red. After a while, your anger would abate and your natural ground color would return. However, someone looking at your aura for the first time, who did not know what was happening, might assume that your main aura color was orange or red.

Our auras reflect our moods every minute of the day. If you are relaxing peacefully your aura would contain a large amount of green. If you were concentrating on solving a problem at work, your aura, particularly around your head, would be full of yellow.

The quality of the colors reflects our actual mood. An athlete about to attempt a world record would have a large amount of red in his or her aura. But this red would be vibrant, shimmering and pure. Contrast this with someone who is angry and is about to pick a fight with someone else. The red in this case would be dirty, dark and muddy-looking, reflecting the person's feelings of anger and rage.

You can practice reading these reactions with your partner, by having him or her imagine different moods. They will not be able to capture exactly the murkiness in the aura of someone possessed with greed, lust or envy, but this experiment will give you a good idea of the changes that occur inside the aura when someone's emotions become involved.

Seek out opportunities to watch people's auras in different environments. Watch a pianist totally lost in the music he or she is playing. Observe an athlete preparing for a race. See a classroom of people sitting for an exam. One example I particularly love to watch is a choir singing a song they all love. In this example all the individual auras appear to merge above their heads and flow heavenwards in a beautiful white column of pure energy.

Some years ago I was drawing auras at a large exhibition. At the start of the day everyone I saw appeared fresh and excited. As the day went on, I saw more and more tired looking auras, and by the end of the day, the auras appeared frustrated and confused. Everyone at this exhibition was gradually becoming more and more frustrated because they had just a short amount of time to see everything they wanted to, and as the exhibition was crowded they were finding it difficult to do it all. Consequently, as the day went on I was seeing more and more of people's mood auras and less and less of their true auras. It was an interesting experience for me to watch crowd frustration build up in this way.

You can see similar effects at sports games, particularly when the home team is losing.

Every thought creates an effect on the aura. These are known as thought forms. Simple daydreaming has little effect, but important, constructive thoughts can be read very clearly in the aura. Thoughts are more powerful than we sometimes realize. Negative thoughts build up insidiously and over a period of time can create illness in the physical body. This negativity can be seen in the aura as soon as it begins. We all have between fifty and sixty thousand thoughts a day and most of us have no idea how many of these thoughts are positive and how many are negative. Unfortunately, most people think many more negative thoughts than they do positive ones.

This is why affirmations are so valuable. Affirmations are simply positive thoughts that are deliberately placed in the mind. The mind has no idea if a thought is accidental or deliberate. It simply acts on what it receives. It is a good idea to immediately switch any negative thoughts to positive ones whenever you find yourself thinking negatively.

The mind does not even know or care if the affirmation is true or not. For instance, if you are experiencing money problems, you are likely to be thinking a large number of negative thoughts about your situation. The chances are you will be thinking much more about poverty than about wealth. If, in this situation, you said to yourself, "I create prosperity," every time you found yourself thinking negative thoughts about money, your mind would start to think more positively about your financial situation and, in time, you would start creating prosperity. The change in your financial situation might take time to manifest, but the change in your aura would be immediate.

Meanings of the Colors

The mood colors come and go and are not always easy to interpret, particularly when a number of colors are interwoven together in the aura. A striking example of this is when a dark dirty red color is combined with black. Black in the aura is never a good sign, and mixed with red it denotes cruelty, hatred and evil. When people "see red" they are actually "seeing" a dirty, muddy red with plenty of black in it. This negative energy can sometimes be seen as a virtual fire surrounding the person's head. Frequently, after an attack like that, the person will suffer a bad headache.

Red on its own as a mood color simply means vitality and outgoing, positive, happy feelings. It can also denote sexual energy.

Orange denotes feelings and emotions. If the color is clear and pleasant to look at, it shows ambition, a positive outlook, and a sympathetic approach to others. A muddy orange indicates selfishness and pride.

Yellow is always seen as a mood aura when someone is concentrating and using his or her brain. Reading, writing, concentrating, or any other left-brain activity create a yellow mood aura. School teachers would love to see this color inside the auras of all their pupils! Yellow comes and goes rapidly, denoting the rapid changes in our thought patterns.

Green as a mood color can indicate that energy is being drained and that the person needs a good night's rest. If the entire aura becomes suffused with green the person becomes detached and withdrawn from others. This is a temporary situation that's remedied by sufficient rest. A very dark green is a sign of deceit and dishonesty.

When green and blue appear together in a mood aura it is a sign of sympathetic understanding and an intuitive awareness.

Blue as a mood color indicates integrity, sensitivity, positive thoughts, and a desire to progress. Deep blue indicates spirituality and inspiration.

Indigo as a mood color indicates spiritual awareness. The person is questioning things and building up a personal faith or philosophy.

Violet as a mood color reveals someone who is confident in his or her faith and is developing spiritually. It is not surprising that bishops wear purple robes to denote their spiritual calling. Violet usually appears around the edges of a mood aura and seldom takes over the entire aura.

Gray as a mood color reveals someone who is feeling dull or depressed. It indicates a temporary lack of imagination and a conventional, unexciting, even boring, approach. Stress can also cause this color to appear.

Pink as a mood color shows the person is affectionate, kind, and gentle.

Silver and gold are seldom seen as mood colors. When they appear it shows the person is receiving inspirational or intuitive ideas that need to be carefully thought through before being acted upon. It can sometimes indicate that the person has received a sudden flash of brilliance.

White appears as a mood color when the person is experiencing intuitive impressions. A psychic, for example, would have a great deal of white in his or her aura, while picking up impressions clairvoyantly.

Brown in the mood aura indicates someone who wants to dominate the situation, but finds it hard to do so because of an excess of negativity. Small areas of brown indicate someone who is down to earth, but fixed and rigid in his or her outlook. This person is a closed thinker and has no desire to learn new ideas or ways of doing things, and is completely self-contained. People like this can be very boring to others as they are interested only in themselves and want to talk about their favorite subject at great length.

Black is highly negative at any time, but particularly so when it is the color of the mood aura. Usually, it is mixed with another color, and the nature of its negativity is determined from the other color. For instance, red and black indicates hatred, cruelty, and total malevolence. Black and yellow indicates evil thoughts. Black and green indicates envy, avarice, and treachery.

It is difficult to give exact meanings for all of the colors you will see in the aura. This is because we express ourselves in different ways. Greed may show up in one person's aura in a completely different manner than the way it shows up in the aura of someone else. Also, there is an almost infinite variety of shadings and degrees of each color.[1] The best way to learn is by being alert and observing as many auras as you can in as many different situations as possible.

Health in the Aura

A healthy aura glows with life, health and vitality. It proclaims to the world that the person is healthy in mind, body and spirit. If something is wrong in any of these areas it shows up in the aura.

With the exception of accidents, ill health is usually the result of years of negative thinking, and naturally, this shows up in the aura well before it is apparent in the physical body. Mental and emotional factors influence the aura constantly, creating either health or illness, depending on how the person is living his or her life.

Potential illness can be seen by looking at the aura's size, shape, appearance, texture, and color. All of these can be affected by the onset of disease. They often show up in the aura well before the person is aware of any problem. Kirlian photographs of the leaves of plants show discolorations when they are suffering from the early stages of a viral disease, well before this can be detected by any other means.[1]

People who have been suffering from chronic ill health for a long while often have auras that appear grayish brown. The ground color and radiating streamers virtually disappear, but return as these people regain their health. This color also shows in the aura, particularly around the head, with the onset of a migraine headache. In this case it appears to be very gray and thick in texture.

Drugs affect the aura in different ways, changing the subtle vibrations and making the aura appear coarse and unhealthy. Long-term substance abuse can cause permanent changes in the aura, revealing the damage that has occurred in the body.

Damage to the muscles of the body are shown by what appear to be holes in the aura. These holes disappear as the muscle returns to health.

Most health conditions are indicated by a blotchy, spotty area in the etheric body. These can turn into solid areas of an ugly brown or black if the health problem continues for some time. At the same time the rays of energy radiating through the aura become faint and dull.

It is not surprising that the etheric body is affected in this way, for one of its functions is to transmit, receive and store the energies that constantly surround us. When this energy is depleted sickness often occurs. The etheric body is sometimes referred to as the health aura.

Pain reveals itself in many different ways in the aura. Alongside the afflicted area is what appears to be a solid piece of blackness, usually in the etheric body. This often appears as a gray smudge before the person becomes unwell. For instance, if someone is about to get a severe chest cold a gray smudge will appear in the chest area of the aura. Once the cold is established the gray will become darker and darker until it is finally black.

Pain is shown by a small aura that almost appears turned in on itself. This denotes the lack of energy the person has. The degree of pain is indicated by how extreme this reaction is. Someone who suffers from occasional migraines will experience a condensed, turned-in aura shortly before and during the migraine attack. The aura will expand to its normal size again as soon as the migraine has passed.

Someone who has to live with chronic pain will have a permanently shrunken aura and the colors will be subdued and dull. The area that is causing the pain will be indicated by blackness in the aura.

I know a lady who has suffered from constant pain inside her mouth for some twenty years. The pain is mainly on the underside of her tongue. Doctors have been unable to help her. She is allergic to pain killers and experiences relief only when she hypnotizes herself. Her aura flickers as if the energy is constantly coming and going. In fact, the pain appears to come and go in constant waves, and her aura reflects this. The blackness in the aura around her mouth appears almost like a piece of coal.

The aura can also be used to heal. I believe that most spiritual and magnetic healers are using their auras to at least some extent in their healing work. There are large energy centers, similar to the chakras, in our hands that can provide strength and healing energies to people who need it. In a sense these healers are transmitting magnetic energy to the people they are healing. Kirlian photography has demonstrated the change in coloration and appearance of the healer's aura when he or she is engaged in healing. An American researcher reported that the aura of a spiritual healer called Ethel de Loach changed the moment she began using her healing powers. The blue streams of light that surrounded her hands while resting changed into a vivid orange glow.[2]

Healing by sending prayers also uses the aura. By combining thought with feeling and emotion the person doing the praying is able to send vibrations directly from his or her aura to the aura of the person they are praying for.

In his book, *A Priest and the Paranormal*, Jack Wellman describes how he does not always need to touch a person when healing with the laying on of hands as he is able to "stroke" the aura with his hands while praying. He describes the aura as possessing a "resilience or sponginess." He also says that people's auras often expand towards the end of his healing.[3] Mr. Wellman is not always able to see the aura, but can always feel it while performing his healing work.

Many aura healers work in a similar way by sending healing thoughts directly to the auras of their patients. They also concentrate on specific colors to build up their own auras, and then transfer these to their patients. The whole process is mental and spiritual.

In 1915 Swami Panchadasi published his book *The Human Aura*.[4] In it he gives an example of this form of aura healing. "A nervous, unstrung patient may be treated by bathing him mentally in a flood of violet or lavender auric color; while a tired, used up, fatigued person may be invigorated by flooding him with bright reds, followed by bright, rich yellows, finishing the treatment with a steady flow of warm orange color." The process is concluded by visualizing a Great White Light. "This will leave the patient in an inspired, exalted, illuminated state of mind and soul, which will be of great benefit to him, and will also have the effect of reinvigorating the healer by cosmic energy."[5]

Patients are also frequently instructed in color breathing. They visualize the colors that are lacking or depleted and take deep breaths of these colors, ideally outdoors in fresh air and sunlight. People who are anemic, for instance, would be told to visualize the color red while doing their color exercises.

It is best to start color breathing by relaxing comfortably and taking several deep breaths. Close your eyes and then breathe in the color you desire. Visualize the area that needs to be healed, and see it restored to good health. Slowly exhale while you focus on this thought. Repeat two or three more times. Do this several times a day until you achieve the results you desire.

The Rosicrucians have a method of color healing that I can vouch for from my own experience. If someone is experiencing emotional problems, simply imagine this person surrounded by a protective shield of pure pink, and send this thought to him or her with love. When someone is feeling depleted physically, do the same thing, but visualize the person surrounded by a vibrant, bright orange color.[6] A friend of mine became totally depressed when her partner suddenly left without warning. For several weeks I visualized her surrounded in a healing aura of pink, and watched her start to climb out of the depression and start life anew.

How can color healing work? As you know, every part of the body is controlled by a different color and every color has a different vibration. If part of the body is not well, an infusion of the correct color that vibrates to the same rate as the diseased organ will help in effecting a cure.

Color healing uses the colors of the rainbow to help restore balance and harmony to the aura. Sunlight, of course, has been used for healing purposes from time immemorial. This is white light. The color healer uses light and color together to either provide a color that is lacking in the aura, or to provide the complementary color if someone is suffering from an excess of one color. The complementary colors are:

Red – Blue
Orange – Violet
Yellow – Violet
Green – Magenta
Blue – Red
Indigo – Orange
Violet – Yellow

Green is the natural healing color. It is restful, peaceful, and soothing, but also increases the vitality and strengthens the nervous system. Green is considered the most restful color for the human eye. Consequently, it is the most commonly used color in color healing. However, all the other colors have their uses as well.

Food and Drink

Colors that are lacking, or present in small quantities, in the aura can be helped by eating foods of the right color. In the East, the cook usually tries to provide the colors of the first four chakras as this creates a meal that is attractive to look at and is easy to digest.[7]

Red foods include meat, beets, peppers, grapes and all red-skinned fruit.

Orange foods include oranges, carrots, pumpkins, sweet corn and apricots.

Yellow foods include butter, egg yolks, grapefruit, melons and yellow-skinned fruits and vegetables.

Green foods include green vegetables and fruits.

Blue foods include blueberries and plums. (Incidentally, blue is a natural appetite suppressant.)

Indigo foods include grapes, plums, blueberries and blackberries.

Violet foods include eggplants, grapes, blackberries and purple broccoli.

You can also "charge" water with the color you require. To do this, simply put the water into a glass container of the correct color and leave it on a window ledge, or anywhere else where it will be exposed to light, for four hours. This water will last for two weeks if you keep it in a refrigerator. If you do not have a container of the correct color, place a sheet of colored glass between the container and the light source. The charged water can be used internally and externally.

Music

Music can be very soothing to the aura. The best music for this purpose is slow and gentle. Baroque and meditation music are ideal. The aura responds to these types of music and expands as it gains energy. Loud, discordant music has the opposite effect on the aura.

Every note in music relates to a color and also has an effect on the aura. Paracelsus, the famous sixteenth-century occultist, practiced musical healing and prescribed specific compositions for certain disorders.[8] Paracelsus believed the body was composed of two substances, one visible and the other invisible. He believed he could heal sick people by reharmonizing these two substances by bringing them into contact with healthy people.

Each color has a part to play in color healing. The color can be applied in many ways, ranging from visualization, to rays of light, a drink, or even a gemstone of the right color.

Red

Red stimulates and excites. Consequently, it should never be used on its own, and is normally followed by blue or green. Red releases adrenaline, stimulates the circulation of blood, and restores lost vitality. In laboratory tests it was found that people can increase the power of their muscles by fifty percent while under a saturated red light, compared to their strength while under a more peaceful color.[9]

Orange

Orange is a stimulating, invigorating color that creates a feeling of contentment and well-being. It strengthens the pancreas, spleen and lungs. Consequently, it helps alleviate bronchitis, asthma, and winter influenza and colds.

Yellow

Yellow is a cheerful, mentally stimulating color that raises the spirits and can alleviate depression. It works primarily on the nervous system, but also gives good muscle tone and general vitality. It can be used for constipation, flatulence, dyspepsia and heart palpitations. However, it must be used with care as too much yellow can cause diarrhea. Yellow also helps spread energies to all of the chakras.

Green

Green, being the color of harmony and healing, is a natural tonic. It relieves stress and tension, and stimulates the pituitary gland. A gentle green light can help relieve headaches. Green has always been considered a color of fertility.

Blue

Blue possesses antiseptic and astringent qualities. It is calm and peaceful and is useful for any inflamed or feverish conditions because of its cooling effect. As it controls the throat chakra, blue is very useful for colds, sore throats, and goiter. It is also useful for cuts, abrasions, burns and rheumatism.

Indigo

Indigo has cooling properties. It works on the physical, emotional and spiritual levels. It reduces bleeding, and is frequently used for problems with the ears, eyes and nose.

Violet

Violet works on the highest levels and is very useful for stress and strain. It works well in curing insomnia, eye problems and mental disorders.

As well as the colors, the patient must maintain a positive attitude. As you know, our moods show up in the aura, and positive thoughts and feelings have a beneficial effect on our health. Negative thoughts and feelings do the opposite.

Aura Protection

There is a simple procedure to follow if you feel that your auric energies are being depleted.[10] This depletion can be caused in many ways, ranging from stress, overwork, ill health or by someone else draining your energy. Whenever you need to protect yourself simply make circles out of your thumbs and forefingers and interlock them (Figure 7.1). Imagine yourself surrounded and protected by pure white light. In a matter of

Figure 7.1.
Aura Protection procedure

moments you will feel revitalized. It is better to treat the cause rather than the result, but sometimes there is no alternative. If your partner or your boss is the person causing the aura depletion, you should use this form of protection every day, maybe even several times a day.

You can avoid harmful stress by imagining yourself wrapped in a beautiful rainbow that spirals around your body from head to toe. This rainbow will deflect any stress, give you energy, and also make you more outgoing and popular.[11]

Another method is to simply imagine yourself surrounded by pure white light. This is known as a protective aura. No matter what stress or tension comes at you, the white light deflects it off and away, leaving you calm, relaxed and stress-free. This white light is a form of "spiritual armor" that can be used anytime you feel the need for psychic protection.[12]

Naturally, prevention is better than cure. If you see any health indications in your own aura take whatever steps are necessary to correct the problem. Ensure that there is love in your life. There is convincing evidence that elderly people who live on their own, but have a pet to love and look after, live longer than people who don't. Pay some attention to physical fitness. Avoid harmful stress. Make sure you get enough sleep, and take a vacation every now and again. Have fun. Often adults take life far too seriously. Every now and again do something extravagant or silly just for the sake of it.

If you look after your body, it will look after you, and the beneficial results will show up clearly in your aura.

8

Self-Improvement & Your Aura

Hopefully, we are all progressing as we make our way through this particular incarnation. For most of us, this progression is done in a rather haphazard way. For many people motivation for further education seems to disappear as soon as they leave school or college. The same thing applies to physical fitness. People who excelled in sporting activities in their youth frequently become couch potatoes, watching other athletes perform, and fail to keep themselves in good shape. Every now and again a "couch potato" will become motivated to exercise and get into shape again. Former students sometimes carry on with their education in later life, but sadly, these transformations happen infrequently.

These are the obvious areas, of course, and generally these people know that they should be doing something that is mentally or physically stimulating.

It is not quite so easy to discover the need to develop in other areas of our lives. We may feel a vague sense that we are not doing all we could, or should, with our lives, but most of us try to ignore that faint sense of unease at the back of our minds.

Fortunately, it is a comparatively simple matter to determine what we should be doing, and where we should be going, by looking at our own auras.

We start by looking at the ground color. Is it vibrant and radiantly alive, or is it dull and withdrawn? Does it reach out into the world with an appearance of optimism and enthusiasm? Or is it perhaps retreating as we hide from life?

It can be a chastening experience to do this. At one time, when my children were young, I was working three jobs to make ends meet. It meant I was spending very little time at home with my family, but the bills were being paid and we had a little money in the bank for emergencies.

One evening, I noticed that the aura around a person I worked with was extremely dull. When I mentioned it, he told me that he was always exhausted and didn't know how much longer he could keep up his part-time job. As I was feeling very tired myself that night, I immediately looked at my own aura and was horrified to find that it had a grayish tinge to it and it was only half its normal size. My aura was telling me that I was overdoing things and that it was time to make changes in my life.

It was a simple matter for me to check out my aura, but I had neglected to do so until it was almost too late. I am certain that if I had continued with the three jobs my health would have been affected. Needless to say, ever since that experience, I have checked my aura regularly.

It also pays to check the coloration of your ground color. Our emotions affect our auras all the time. Maybe it doesn't matter too much if your ground color occasionally becomes suffused with a dirty green tinge when you are envious of someone else's success. However, you must learn to handle this destructive emotion if you find the envious green is there most of the time.

RED

If you have a red ground color you should be ambitious, determined, outgoing and optimistic. If you feel listless, apathetic and introverted, you are not doing what you should be doing. (Remember that your ground color reveals what you should be doing with your life.) There could be any number of reasons for this. You may simply have burned yourself out by not allowing enough time for rest and relaxation. You may be doing a job that you are not suited for or do not enjoy. Relationships may not be working as well as they should be. If you find it hard to work out what the problem is, use a pendulum to find the answer. Ask the pendulum questions that can be answered with a "yes" or a "no." "Am I happy in my work?" "Is my relationship progressing?" You may be surprised with the answers you get. Keep on asking questions until you find out the area or areas that are causing you difficulty.

If your red ground color is not as it should be, there are a number of things that you can do to restore it to its natural, vibrant form.

You can increase the amount of physical exercise you do. Start going for walks. It will give you time to think and give you beneficial exercise at the same time. Your walks should be at least twenty minutes long, and preferably twice that.

Maybe you could take up a competitive sport of some sort. Reds enjoy competing. Keep in mind though, that it is not always necessary to win. With a red ground color, your natural position is at the top. If you have a strong desire to be first in everything you do, you may find it better to choose some non-competitive physical activity, as the purpose of the exercise is to achieve physical fitness, rather than to win gold medals. However, if your goal in life is to compete at the Olympics, ignore this and move on to the next paragraph.

You can set yourself some ambitious goals. Red is an ambitious, succeeding color. Choose something really worthwhile, something that will stretch you, something that you'll be proud of achieving. As you achieve success and recognition, your red ground color will expand and glow.

You should mix with positive-minded, successful people who can stimulate and encourage you. You should avoid small-minded or negative people who will try to hold you back from achieving your goals.

ORANGE

With an orange ground color you should be easy to get along with, and be a cooperative, kind, caring person. If you feel that you are confused, frustrated or not able to express yourself in the manner you desire, there are a number of things you can do to enhance and expand your aura.

You need to feel that you are doing something productive and useful. Look around and see what you could do that would allow you to feel useful. One lady I know took it upon herself to make sure that the office supplies in her office were always adequate. Previously, people kept complaining about the lack of pens, laser cartridges, drawing pins, etc. She received no acknowledgment or thanks for taking on this task, but enjoyed a quiet sense of satisfaction for doing something useful.

You should accept yourself for who you are, and achieve pleasure and satisfaction out of nurturing and caring for others. Your greatest satisfactions will come when you feel emotionally fulfilled. You should mix with like-minded, caring, intuitive, humanitarian people.

You may feel overly sensitive and appear shy and hesitant. If this is the case, you need to learn to channel this sensitivity into humanitarian areas and develop your talents at working with others. As your sensitivity gradually becomes channeled into other areas, your confidence and satisfaction with life will grow.

YELLOW

With yellow as your ground color you should be getting along well with others and be adept at expressing yourself in some sort of way, ideally creatively. You should be warming others with your cheerfulness and ability to charm and captivate. If you feel that this is not the case, there are a number of areas you can work on.

You should work on expressing yourself more to others. Your gifts of verbal expression can help others as you have the ability to brighten any gathering. You should be using your voice in some manner in your working life. A sole-charge position is not for you. You would be much happier as a teacher, salesperson, consultant, counselor, or any other position where your voice is being used.

Beneath the bright, cheery exterior you may feel overly sensitive. Work on developing a thicker skin, and use your sense of humor to deflect any attacks.

You need to avoid a frivolous, casual approach to life. With a yellow ground color you become enthusiastic about so many different things that it is often difficult for other people to keep up. They are likely to regard you as a dilettante and not take any of your ideas seriously. If you are having difficulties in this area, you can eliminate them by taking on a mentally stimulating or creative project and carrying it through to completion.

You have a good brain and use it well, but you may feel as if you are not doing as much with your life as you could be doing. If this is the case, choose a subject that interests you and determine to become an expert in it. Years ago, I heard a speaker say that if you spent an hour a night studying a subject that interested you, you would be an expert in that subject in less than a year. Choose a subject that is worthy of your ability and take it as far as you can.

GREEN

If you have green as your ground color you should be a caring, benevolent humanitarian. You are likely to be a compassionate person who enjoys helping others. You also should be stable, conscientious and responsible. If you are not doing these things it will be reflected in the appearance of your aura.

You can enhance the look of your aura by actively seeking out opportunities to help others. This can be done in a very small way, such as doing the shopping for a neighbor who is ill. It can also be done in much larger ways, such as taking on the responsibility for a humanitarian organization, or perhaps righting something in your community that you consider wrong.

You may feel hemmed in and restricted. This can be extremely frustrating, as everywhere you turn there are more and more limitations. Look at yourself and see if you are being too rigid and stubborn. You might need to lighten up and relax more. Accept that we all have restrictions and limitations, and work within them.

You will find it helpful to work on a program of self-development, taking on new challenges and extending yourself in some way.

If you are feeling bored or restricted you should spend time with caring, understanding people who will open your mind to new challenges and opportunities.

You have the ability to work hard and long to achieve your goals. You have great persistence and determination. Use these attributes wisely and achieve something worthwhile.

BLUE

With blue as your ground color you should be adventurous, enthusiastic, creative, imaginative and perceptive. You should feel forever young, with opportunities everywhere you look. You need to be mentally stimulated and enjoy meeting people from every type of culture.

Some blues find it hard to relax and need to learn to take time out to unwind and restore themselves. If you find it hard to relax, you can become emotionally stressed. You do not find many people who use their blue ground color negatively.

However, there is a tendency for some to take on too many different activities. When they do, they scatter their energies over too wide an area. These people need to learn to concentrate on a handful of projects and to complete them before going on to something new.

You may feel impatient and restless. This can make it difficult to finish one task before moving on to the next.

If you feel that your progress is erratic or that you overindulge too often, look back and see how much you have achieved with all the wonderful gifts you have been given. If you use your gifts wisely you have the opportunity to make enormous progress in any field that interests you.

INDIGO

People who have indigo as their ground color are usually responsible, self-reliant, caring people. Other people are attracted to them because they sense their humanitarian qualities.

If you are not manifesting the positive attributes of your indigo ground color you probably need to learn to trust others and act more on your feelings. These feelings will help you become more attuned with both yourself and others.

People with indigo as their ground color usually need to make time for play and relaxation. They can sometimes become so immersed in helping others that they fail to sense when it is time to let go and unwind.

You may find that you are overly critical of yourself and others. You may expect perfection. If this is the case, you will need to learn to relax and realize that you are not responsible for everything. Let go of some of the less important things and use the time you gain for creative activities and for quality time with friends and loved ones.

VIOLET

People with a violet ground color are sensitive, spiritual and intuitive. They are sensitive to other people's needs and encourage and nurture others in a quiet, reserved way. Their strong faith supports and sustains them in difficult times. They rely on themselves, often finding it hard to ask others for help.

If you are not reflecting the positive traits of your violet ground color, your aura will appear limp and dull, and hug your body closely. Fortunately, it is not difficult to bring it back to its full glory.

If you feel that other people are insensitive to your feelings, work on expressing yourself more clearly.

Many people with a violet ground color find it hard to express their innermost feelings and hold themselves back.

A few people with a violet ground color are overly introspective and find it hard to relate to others. If you feel that this describes you, be aware that you have a great deal to offer. You are depriving others, as well as yourself, when you hold back and fail to communicate.

You may find it hard to fit in with others. You may prefer to do things your own way and not be prepared to try other approaches. Your unique approach works well for you, but may not be suitable for others. Be aware of other people's needs and try to become more adaptable.

SILVER

People with a silver ground color are idealistic, inspirational and intuitive. They are honorable, honest and trusting. They believe in themselves and always manage to find the best in other people.

If you are not expressing the positive characteristics of your silver ground color your aura will appear dull, gray and lifeless. You can enhance the quality of your aura in many ways.

Become more aware of your own special gifts and attributes. Develop your self-esteem. Trust your intuition. You may need to push yourself a bit more. You are full of great ideas, but sometimes find it difficult to make them happen. Keep on dreaming the great dreams, but complete the exercise by setting constructive goals, making a plan of action, and finally making it happen. As you do this, the quality of your aura will amaze you.

You may suffer from nervous tension. This can make it hard for other people to get close to you. You will find it beneficial to learn how to relax by using meditation, yoga, or self-hypnosis.

GOLD

If you have a gold ground color you should be idealistic, responsible, extremely capable and successful. You have high ideals and goals, and can make them happen. You are a natural leader, being able to inspire others with your charisma and energy.

It is rare to find a negative person with a gold ground color. However, if your dreams have been shattered you may temporarily find yourself seeking a quiet shelter while you restore your energies and prepare to start again. You can be your own worst enemy when things do not work out the way you intended. You expect much more of yourself than you do from others, and can be overly hard on yourself. Recognize that everyone makes mistakes, even you, and that mistakes do not matter as long as we learn from them. Take whatever time it takes to restore yourself, then make more big plans before going out to reach for the stars once again.

PINK

With pink as your ground color you should be affectionate, loving and caring. However, despite this gentle appearance you are also prepared to stand up for your beliefs and put your point of view across. You are happiest when you are free to be yourself and have time to love and nurture the people you care for.

If you are not expressing the positive characteristics of your ground color the pink will appear washed out and empty.

If you are feeling dependent on others, take steps to assert your independence. Take up a new hobby or interest. Move outside your comfort zone and do something that you have always wanted to do. Your friends and family may be surprised, but will give you their support when you tell them exactly why you are doing it.

If you feel over-burdened with responsibilities and people are trying to put all their problems on your shoulders, consider it a good opportunity to learn to delegate. This is also an excellent time to finally learn to say "no." You find it hard to turn other people down. Recognize that you have needs of your own that need to be satisfied, also.

A few people with a pink ground color are timid and scared to take risks. If this applies to you, you will have to take steps to develop your confidence and learn to express yourself comfortably.

BRONZE

If you have bronze as your ground color, you are gentle, caring, enthusiastic, and quietly determined. You are happiest when helping others, but often do this in a quiet, almost detached manner, as you need to be emotionally independent.

Most people with a bronze ground color are positive and happy. However, you are likely to feel negative when you feel that you are being taken for granted by others. When you are aware of this, withdraw a little bit and make time to do something for yourself.

You may sometimes underestimate your capabilities and put other people ahead of yourself. If you feel this is the case, take steps to develop your confidence and self-esteem. You may find a course in public speaking or assertiveness training helpful.

You may feel easily hurt. You are sensitive and caring and it can be hard when other people take advantage of your good nature. You must learn to be selfless, so that your giving is done with no thought of any return. This is a difficult lesson to learn, but the ultimate rewards can be unbelievable.

WHITE

With white as your ground color, you are pure, individualistic, creative and have a strong need for time on your own to grow in knowledge and wisdom.

When you are not expressing the positive characteristics of your ground color your aura will appear blotchy, almost as if there are holes in it. It will also condense and hug your body.

If you feel lonely at times, it is up to you to go out and make friends. To make friends you need to be a friend first. You do not need to give up your individuality to have friends. You can apportion your time to maintain your necessary periods of solitude and quietness.

A few people with a white ground color are egocentric and think only of their own needs. It is not surprising that these people feel isolated and alone. These people need to become aware of other people's needs and learn to help others.

You may need to learn how to use your time constructively. You enjoy new ideas and concepts and long for time to work on them. Simplify your lifestyle, if you can, to give you the necessary freedom to explore and develop these ideas.

The Chakras

It is not easy to see the chakras in your own aura. You will be able to do this if you are fortunate enough to be able to see your aura clearly in a mirror. Most of us have to determine the well-being of our own chakras in other ways. Feeling them is a good method for many people. Or perhaps a friend could look at your chakras and advise you.

Pendulum Method

With the pendulum method you need to sit down quietly by yourself and ask the pendulum questions about each chakra. Start with the root chakra and work your way up to the crown chakra.

"Is my root chakra healthy?" is the first question to ask your pendulum. If the answer is positive, you can then continue asking questions relating to self-improvement. If the answer is negative, you can ask questions about restoring this chakra to good health. We will assume that the pendulum gave a negative answer to the first question.

"Is my root chakra over-stimulated?" you then ask. If the answer is positive you can take steps to reduce the over-activity.

If you receive a negative response to this question, follow it by asking if the chakra is under-stimulated. Again, if this answer is positive, you can do something to restore it to balance.

Ask the same questions of all the chakras. Once you have finished, you can then take whatever steps are necessary to restore your chakras to balance.

Meditation Method

Another method is through meditation. Sit down quietly somewhere in a comfortable place where you will not be disturbed. I often do this while sitting under my Oracle Tree.[1] An oracle tree is simply a tree that attracts you and becomes your friend. It is highly restoring to your body and soul to spend time sitting under your personal oracle tree. You do not choose an oracle tree for yourself. It finds you. You have a duty to look after the ground around your oracle tree, and in return the tree will give you comfort and support.

When indoors, I select a comfortable chair and disconnect the phone for the length of the meditation.

After going through a progressive relaxation exercise I picture each of the chakras in turn, mentally feeling them in my body. I then ask myself the same questions I ask the pendulum and my body responds with the answer.

The advantage of this method over the pendulum is that I can mentally send messages to any chakra asking it to speed up and become more alive, or, alternatively, to slow down and become balanced again.

Music Method

Music can soothe and restore us with its pleasing harmonies and melodies. The right music is recuperative, restores our energy and vitality, and increases our enjoyment of life. Naturally, the wrong sort of music can be harmful and fill us with anger and rage. Hal A. Lingerman, in his book *The Healing Energies of Music*, wrote that destructive music can "affect your entire aura, making you feel psychically torn apart, fragmented, frightened, combative, isolated, tense and aimless."[2] Music has always been used to incite people to action. Just imagine the power that drums must have had—and still have—for the Native Americans.

Music that is soothing to me may not necessarily do the same thing for you. Inspirational music can restore and invigorate your soul. I'll never forget coming out into the street after hearing Beethoven's *9th Symphony* for the first time. I was inspired, uplifted and in tune with the infinite. Music can also be extremely useful in restoring balance to your chakras.

Next time you listen to music, relax comfortably, close your eyes and ask yourself where in your body you feel the music. It is likely to be in one of your chakras. This is an indication that this particular chakra is being affected by the music, which is harmonizing your body and returning it to balance.

As a general rule, different instruments have a different effect on each part of the body.

The Physical Body is affected by brass instruments and percussion.

The Emotional Body is affected by woodwind and string instruments.

The Mental Body is stimulated by string instruments.

The Spiritual Body is affected by harps, organs, high strings and wind chimes.[3]

Dr. John Diamond, in his book *Your Body Doesn't Lie*, writes: "Surrounded by the right sounds, we all can be invigorated, energized and balanced." He also claims that music can help "the prevention of illness at the pre-physical, energy-imbalance level."[4]

Recommended Music for the Root Chakra

The root chakra is frequently over-stimulated. Relating to the color red, this often leads to domination, aggression, possessiveness and other extremes of behavior. It can also be extremely passionate and emotional, creating rapidly changing moods.

All of this can be quieted down and balanced by meditation, long walks in the country or by the seashore and by listening to gentle music. Suitable pieces to listen to are: *Air on the G String* by Johann Sebastian Bach, *Canon in D* by Johann Pachelbel, *The Four Seasons* by Antonio Vivaldi, *Concerto for Flute and Harp* by Wolfgang Amadeus Mozart, and the *Holberg Suite* by Edvard Grieg.

If the root chakra is under-stimulated there will be a lethargic, apathetic approach to life. The person will be listless and find everything too much effort. There will be little or no interest in sex or entertainment.

Obviously, in this case, the person needs to gain more energy. This can be achieved by encouraging the person to engage in physical activities and to spend happy times with cheerful friends. There is a wealth of music the person can listen to. Almost any brass band music would be suitable, but especially the upbeat, happy pieces. Other pieces include: *Pomp and Circumstance March No. 1* ("Land of Hope and Glory") by Sir Edward Elgar, the "Triumphal March" from *Aida* by Giuseppe Verdi, "The Stars and Stripes Forever" by John Philip Sousa, "Marche Slave" by Peter Ilyitch Tchaikovsky, "March Militaire" by Franz Schubert, the "Turkish March" from the *Ruins of Athens* by Ludwig van Beethoven, and the "Radetsky March" by Johann Strauss the Senior.

Recommended Music for the Sacral Chakra

The Sacral Chakra relates to balance as it lies between red (physical) and yellow (mental). Consequently, when this chakra is over-stimulated it will tend to reflect the negative qualities of both red and yellow. This can come out as anger, recklessness, unfair or vicious criticism, and a total lack of responsibility.

This chakra can be brought back into balance by allowing time for the person to think things through. A long soak in a warm bath can do wonders in restoring balance to the sacral chakra. Suitable music includes: *Two Concertos for Two Pianos* by Johann Sebastian Bach, Prelude to *Rosamunde* by Franz Schubert, the

Harp Concerto by George Frideric Handel, and any of John Dowland's lute music.

If the sacral chakra is under-stimulated the person will feel timid, fearful and indecisive. His or her imagination is likely to run riot with imagined fears and difficulties.

The chakra can be brought back into balance by encouraging self-confidence and self-reliance. He or she should be encouraged to seek new challenges and to achieve them. Suitable music includes: the *Egmont Overture* by Ludwig van Beethoven, the Prelude to *Lohengrin* (Act 3) by Richard Wagner, *Piano Concerto No. 1* by Johannes Brahms, the last movement of *Symphony No. 3* (Organ) by Camille Saint-Saëns, and the last movement of *Symphony No. 5* by Peter Ilyitch Tchaikovsky.

Recommended Music for the Solar Chakra

The Solar Chakra is related to the mind and nervous system. When it is over-stimulated it reflects the negative qualities of failing to complete projects, scattering energy, and leading a superficial life. Quick progress will be followed by periods of lethargy, and the person is likely to be highly erratic. Living in the imagination will be preferable to reality, and the person is likely to construct elaborate dreams that never happen.

To restore balance to an over-stimulated solar chakra the person will need to learn to think first before expressing opinions, and to ensure that he or she is honest in thought and action. Suitable music includes: *Appalachian Spring* by Aaron Copland, the

Oboe Concertos by Antonio Vivaldi, "Evening Star" (from *Tannhauser*) by Richard Wagner, and *Clair de lune* by Claude Debussy.

If the solar chakra is under-stimulated the person is likely to whine, criticize and gossip. He or she is likely to engage in frivolous, superficial activities and be deceitful, selfish and egotistical. These negative traits can be eliminated by learning to spread cheerfulness and enthusiasm to others. This is not an easy thing to do as it involves a total change in outlook. The person will benefit by periods of soul-searching where he or she can analyze past patterns of behavior and see what mistakes have been made. Suitable music includes: *Water Music* by George Frideric Handel, *Violin Concerto* by Johannes Brahms, *Concerto for Three Violins and Orchestra* by Georg Philipp Telemann, as well as *The Well-Tempered Clavier* and the *Brandenburg Concertos*, both by Johann Sebastian Bach.

Recommended Music for the Heart Chakra

The Heart Chakra relates to healing, nature, balance and a sense of purpose. When this chakra is over-stimulated the person will have difficulties in handling change and will have a deep need for security and safety. This can lead to problems in trying anything new or different. I know a man who refuses to eat any meat other than chicken. As a child his mother indulged him by letting him eat whatever he wanted, and now, in his forties, he will not try anything different. When this chakra is over-stimulated the person can be extremely stubborn and rigid.

To restore balance to the heart chakra these people need to widen their horizons and realize that there are other viewpoints that may be as good—or sometimes better—than their own. When they achieve this, they will be able to help others much more effectively than before and achieve greater happiness and satisfaction in their lives. Suitable music includes: *Pictures at an Exhibition* by Modest Mussorgsky, *Romeo and Juliet Overture* by Peter Ilyitch Tchaikovsky, *Pines of Rome* by Ottorino Respighi, the *Peer Gynt Suite* by Edvard Grieg, *Finlandia* by Jean Sibelius, and the *Symphony No. 6* ("Pastoral") by Ludwig van Beethoven.

If the Heart Chakra is under-stimulated the person will be afraid to attempt anything and will be envious of other people's success. This can lead to petty-mindedness and even cruelty. To restore balance the person should be encouraged to mix with positive people and to spend time in peaceful surroundings. As he or she learns to deal with unfinished business and to let go of the past, every aspect of his or her life will improve. Suitable music includes: *Piano Concerto No. 2* by Serge Rachmaninoff, *Warsaw Concerto* by Richard Addinsell, *Toccata and Fugue in D*, and *Jesu, Joy of Man's Desiring* by Johann Sebastian Bach, *Light Cavalry Overture* by Franz von Suppé, and the *Piano Concerto in A* by Edvard Grieg.

Recommended Music for the Throat Chakra

The Throat Chakra relates to thought. It is curious by nature and wants to know everything. It is expansive and needs to grow and move forward. When this chakra is over-stimulated the person becomes impatient and irresponsible. He or she overindulges in a constant search for vicarious pleasure and stimulation. To restore balance the person should learn to use his or her time wisely, and to think before acting. Suitable music includes: *The Beatitudes* by César Franck, *Grande Polonaise* by Frédéric Chopin, *Violin Concerto* by Max Bruch, *Piano Concerto* by Edvard Grieg, and the *Cello Concerto* by Antonín Dvorák.

When the throat chakra is under-stimulated the person will be lethargic, apathetic, lazy and self-indulgent. To restore balance the person should seek out a worthwhile project that he or she sees as being exciting and different. Suitable music includes: *Piano Concerto No. 5* ("the Emperor") by Ludwig van Beethoven, *The Joy of Life Symphony* by Alfred Hill, *Piano Concerto No. 3* by Joseph Haydn, *Concerto for Organ, Timpani and Strings* by Francis Poulenc, *Panis Angelicus* by César Franck, John Philip Sousa's marches, and *Die Fledermaus Overture* by Johann Strauss.

Recommended Music for the Brow Chakra

The Brow Chakra relates to spiritual understanding, love and humanitarian pursuits. It aids self-knowledge and intuition, and also combines our physical and spiritual natures. It appreciates beauty. When this chakra is over-stimulated the person becomes a meddlesome busybody, creating chaos instead of harmony, and finding it impossible to help others or him or herself. To restore balance these people need time by themselves in aesthetically attractive surroundings to relax and make future plans. They may need to learn to control stress and tension. Suitable music includes: *Prelude* to *Rosamunde* by Franz Schubert, *Two Concertos for Two Pianos* by Johann Sebastian Bach, *Symphony No. 6* by Ludwig van Beethoven, *Concerto for Flute and Harp* by Wolfgang Mozart, *Air on the G String* by Johann Sebastian Bach, and the *Harp Concerto* by George Frideric Handel.

If the brow chakra is under-stimulated the person is likely to withdraw from life and refuse to take on or handle any responsibility. The person is likely to become forgetful, careless with details and intolerant. He or she will be demanding, disapproving and supercilious. To restore balance these people need to spend time in light-hearted fun activities with people they love. They need to learn to let go of past hurts and grievances and to live in the present. They also need to feel needed by others. Suitable music includes: *Trumpet Voluntary* by Jeremiah Clarke, *A Lincoln Portrait* by Aaron Copland, *Finlandia* by Jean Sibelius, *Pope Marcellus Mass* by Giovanni Palestrina, *Symphony No. 3* ("Organ Symphony") by Camille Saint-Saëns, and *Concierto de Aranjuez* by Rodrigo.

Recommended Music for the Crown Chakra

The Crown Chakra represents our higher natures and aspirations. It relates to spirituality, intuition and the desire to know and understand the hidden truths.

It is unusual for this chakra to be over-stimulated. When it is, the person is likely to live in a dream world of his or her own making, and be unable to separate this from reality. This retreat into fantasy frequently makes it impossible for the person to relate to others, and in fact, others are usually condemned because of their lack of perfection. To restore balance to this chakra the person needs to learn balance. They need time on their own for spiritual and metaphysical pursuits, but also need to mix with others at a lighter level. They have the ability to delight, charm and captivate others when they set their minds on it, but may need to force themselves to do this. Suitable music includes: *Symphony No. 2* by Gustav Mahler, *St. Matthew Passion* by Johann Sebastian Bach, *Florida Suite* by Frederick Delius, *Symphony in D Minor* by César Franck, *Piano Concerto No. 1* by Frédéric Chopin, *Ode to St. Cecilia* by George Frideric Handel, and *Rapsodie Espagnole* by Maurice Ravel.

When the crown chakra is under-stimulated the person will be introspective, aloof, proud and arrogant. He or she will put people off with a condescending, superior air. To restore balance the person needs to "lighten up" by indulging in fun activities simply for the pleasure of it. He or she also needs to learn to relate to others at their level and to not expect perfection from everyone. Suitable music includes: *Keltic Sonata* by Edward MacDowell, *Symphony in C* by Georges Bizet, *Guitar Concerto* by Heitor Villa-Lobos, and *Symphony No. 5* by Ludwig van Beethoven.

Magnetic Development

Clairvoyant skills are stimulated in the East by the use of a bar magnet.[5] To do this you need a bar magnet. A horseshoe magnet is not suitable. Suspend the magnet and sit under it for up to half an hour (Figure 8.1). You will have to test to determine which polarity of the magnet creates an expanding effect on your consciousness. You will quickly feel uncomfortable and ill at ease if you are sitting under the wrong polarity.

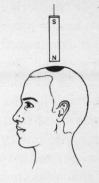

Figure 8.1

Once you have determined this, you will find your sessions under the magnet useful and beneficial. I find it helpful to perform a progressive relaxation exercise while sitting under my magnet. It helps get me sufficiently relaxed and in tune with myself.

People experience the sensations of the magnet in different ways. Some people feel as if the top of their head is expanding or vibrating. Others see colors and shafts of light. You may feel dizzy the first few times you do this experiment.

Persist, and your intuitive skills will gradually develop.

Imprint What You Want in Your Aura

In 1975, Dr. Joe Slate was conducting an experiment at Athens State College in Athens, Georgia. One student was asked to attempt a feat of precognition by projecting his aura energies a few weeks into the future. The student picked up a strong impression of an avalanche that buried buildings and people. The impression he received was so strong that other students in the class could see it in his aura. A few weeks later, in Switzerland, the prediction came true when an avalanche occurred.[6]

You can do exactly the same with your aura. You can either look ahead and see what the next few weeks or months are going to be like for you, or you can set goals for yourself and imprint them in your aura.

Start by sitting down somewhere where you can relax. Close your eyes and drift through your entire life from your earliest memories to the present. You will find that some memories you will linger over, while others are quickly discarded.

Once you reach the present, pause for a moment and reflect on how all of those experiences that you have just relived have made you the person you are today.

Presumably, you are wanting the person you are tomorrow to be a little bit different from the person you are today. Think what you would like to change. Would you like more money? A more satisfying relationship? More free time? A promotion at work?

It makes no difference what it is that you want. Just make sure that you want it enough. Naturally, we would all like a little more money, but do we want it enough to work the extra hours that would be necessary? If you are not prepared to pay the price, forget about that goal and choose something else.

Once you have your goal or goals clearly in your mind, carry on with your life by progressing it into the future. How do you see yourself twelve months from now? Or five years? See yourself as clearly as you can in your mind's eye, happy, contented—and with the goals you set for yourself.

Once this picture is clear in your mind, you can imprint it into your aura. Suppose your goal is to buy a new home within the next twelve months. See yourself, on today's date next year, opening the front door of your new home and walking in. See it as clearly as possible. You want a picture of the house in your mind, so that you can see it and recognize it when you find it.

Make the picture so vivid that you can feel it, see it, and even smell it. Visualize this picture every night when you go to bed. By imprinting your desires into your aura in this way, you will attract the universal forces to you, so that you can make your goal a reality.

Change Your Aura for Success

We all have virtually unlimited potential and can achieve everything we desire, providing we are prepared to set goals, work hard and pay the price.

Look at your aura and see what areas need improving. You may need to change your attitude toward your work. You may need to become more outgoing and friendly. You may have to consciously switch as many of your negative thoughts as you can into positive ones.

You may have bad habits you want to correct. Maybe you want to stop smoking, or change your eating habits.

Your aura will tell you what areas you need to work on. Some may surprise you. I thought I was handling three jobs very well until my aura told me otherwise.

Changing the way you think will transform the look of your aura. Positive thinkers are naturally optimistic and have large, bright, expansive auras. Their thoughts keep them healthy, motivated and ready for action. If your aura is dull and condensed, read motivational, self-help type books for thirty minutes a day and watch your aura develop to reflect your gradual change in attitude.

One of the things that most amazed me when I first began reading auras for other people was that I usually saw a much more positive and interesting version of their lives than they could accept. This relates to self-image. People with a poor self-image achieve only a fraction of their potential. The potential is revealed in their aura and is visible to anyone who knows how to see it, but these people hold themselves back and block their potential. If you have problems in this area, attend a course on building your self-esteem. It is never too late to change your self-concept and make your dreams come true.

Set some worthwhile goals for yourself. Did you know that a vast majority of the world's population simply drift through life with no goals in mind? Most people put more effort into planning a summer vacation than they do in working out where they want to go in life.

It is not easy to set goals if you have not done it before. But the effort will pay off in many ways. You will have something to aim for, and a sense of direction and purpose. And your aura will reflect all of this, becoming large, expansive, and beautiful.

9

Aura Readings

As you start seeing auras your popularity will increase and people will come to you asking for aura readings. If you decide to give readings, you should always do them with kindness, gentleness and concern. There is certainly a place for brief, "fun" readings, but remember that even with these, people will pay close attention to every word you say.

No matter how thick-skinned or skeptical a person may seem, they will remember—often word for word—the things you tell them in the reading. Consequently, you need to choose your words with great care. Your readings should always emphasize the positive and give the person some ideas to think about, and perhaps work on.

Be careful with health problems that you might see. Unless you are a medical doctor you should avoid giving specific advice on health matters. When I see potential health problems in someone's aura I always suggest that they have a medical checkup. If someone's aura is looking tired or stressed, I will suggest they have a vacation or learn a relaxation technique. However, I would not dream of giving someone advice on how to treat, for instance, an inflamed kidney, as I am not a doctor.

I can help people by balancing their auras, by bolstering their self-esteem and by giving suggestions as to where they should be heading in their life and career. I can give suggestions on how to handle potentially dangerous emotions, negative thoughts, laziness and procrastination, but I cannot make people act on my suggestions.

I do not offer advice unless it is asked for. For instance, I would never walk up to a stranger and comment on something I saw in his or her aura. However, if someone came and asked me for a reading I would give it to the best of my capabilities.

Whenever possible, I draw the aura as I speak. I use an artist's sketch pad and good quality colored pencils. The pencils cannot capture the different shades and texture of each color in the aura, but give the person being read for some idea of the appearance of his or her aura. They also provide something tangible for the person to take away and keep.

I have experimented with felt markers, but feel the colors they produce are too garish to depict something as glorious as an aura. Colored pencils are a long way from being perfect, but they are the best I have found so far. I am anything but an artist, but many of my aura portraits are framed and hanging in pride of place in people's homes around the world. One of my students is a talented artist who does aura portraits using pastels. Her portraits are works of art and the pastels allow her to do incredibly accurate depictions of the aura colors. However, I found that I tended to smudge the portraits with pastels, so I went back to my colored pencils.

The other main advantage of drawing the aura is that people often feel tense and nervous when someone stares intently at them for any length of time. By drawing the aura as I talk, I am not constantly staring at them. Consequently, they relax more, and this allows their true auras to reveal themselves to me.

Most of my readings could be defined as character analyses with suggestions about the future. Here are examples of the two types of readings I do, first a brief, "fun" reading, followed by a more serious, in-depth reading.

Let's suppose I'm doing a brief reading for a twenty-five year old man. We'll assume his aura has a blue ground color with red and violet radiating colors. His aura is average in size. As I am talking with him I notice a great deal of yellow around his head, indicating that he is thinking seriously about what I am saying.

My reading would be something along these lines:

"You have a great deal of blue in your aura and this means that you will always be young at heart. You become very enthusiastic about all sorts of things, but may sometimes find it hard to finish everything you start. It looks as if, at times, you have found yourself in trouble for saying exactly what was on your mind. You are a bit more careful about that sort of thing now. However, people usually know exactly where they stand with you, and that is good. You are basically an honest person.

"You would be happiest working in a field that offered great opportunities and plenty of variety. I don't think you've ever liked being told what to do. If the right opportunity for self-employment came along, you should look at it carefully. Long term, you will either be in a position of great responsibility, or self-employed. You should always aim high. If you aim low, you'll reach your goal, but you will also get there if you set your sights really high. In the past you have tended to underestimate yourself. Think big, bold dreams and then make them happen.

"You were probably called a dreamer at school. At that time, it was probably meant negatively. But you are still a dreamer, and always will be. You should consider that a highly positive trait. After all, nothing would ever happen if someone didn't dream it first. It is part of your charm, and it helps keep you forever young. I wouldn't be at all surprised if you were taking up new interests on the day you died!

"You have powerful red lines radiating through your aura. This means you have a strong sense of responsibility. They also give you ambition and a desire for the power and financial rewards that that responsibility can provide.

"Interestingly enough, though, you also have strong violet lines radiating through your aura. This means you enjoy searching for the hidden truths behind things. You seldom take things at face value because you want to find out for yourself. Violet is a spiritual color and I see you gradually developing this and building up a strong faith or philosophy as you go through life.

"Your greatest successes come through your dealings with others, but you also have a need to spend time on your own, to grow in knowledge and wisdom. I can see your education carrying on for a lifetime. In some ways your education really began once you left school. You have an excellent, receptive mind and you carefully evaluate everything that interests you."

All of this information comes from his ground color and two radiating colors. Naturally, if he were a real person I would be able to include much more. I would be able to comment on the texture of his aura, the quality of the colors, the thought forms, his mood at the time, and his stamina and energy levels. You will notice that I made no mention of the chakras. These have an important part to play in the longer readings, but I usually ignore them when giving quick portraits.

Here is an example of a more in-depth reading. This was given for a forty-year-old woman. She was well groomed and expensively dressed, but her face was one of the saddest I have ever seen.

After greeting her and sitting her down in a comfortable chair, I tried to engage her in small talk for a minute or two to help her relax. However, she was not interested in conversation and told me to "get on with it."

"Certainly," I replied. I picked up my pad and started to draw in her ground color. "Your aura is not as large as it should be," I began. "You have obviously depleted your energies and need some rest. A vacation would do you the world of good." She nodded her head but made no comment. "The ground color of your aura is a beautiful, delicate pink. You are not wearing any pink today, but if you did people would comment on how much that color suits you. Pink is a wonderful color to have as it shows that you are a kind and loving person who enjoys being with the people you love."

She stared hard at me for a few moments while I concentrated on coloring in the ground color. She licked her lips and seemed about to speak, but changed her mind.

"You also would do well in the business world, perhaps in a managerial position. However, I think self-employment would suit you better as you are ambitious, determined and motivated."

"You mean stubborn." She gave a harsh laugh.

I nodded. "In a way, yes. However, you are prepared to listen to all points of view. Once your mind is made up, though, it would be almost impossible for anyone to change it. I would see this as a positive trait in the business world, but it could make life difficult in other areas of your life."

"I'm a tyrant." She said this in a casual, matter-of-fact sort of way.

"That can sometimes be an advantage in the competitive world of business." She gave a deep sigh and I noticed traces of orange appearing in her aura. "You try to hold your emotions back," I continued. "This never works for long, as our emotions always win over logic."

I paused and looked at her radiating colors. They were yellow and green. "You have a wonderful, logical brain," I said as I drew in the yellow lines. "You are a quick thinker and can run rings around most people. Someone would have to get up very early in the morning to put anything across you!"

"They've tried," she admitted, "but I usually win."

"You are happiest when you are learning and you need constant mental stimulation. Any partner, for instance, would have to be your mental equal. In fact, any relationship would have to start on a mental level, and if people failed this test with you, you would totally lose interest.

"All the same, your mind is so quick and so sharp that I'm sure you've made comments at times that you've regretted later."

"Haven't we all?"

"I think so, but you can sometimes be hurtful with what you say, and may not even be aware of it."

Her aura became temporarily suffused with orange. "Let your emotions come out," I said. "You've been holding them back long enough."

Tears came to her eyes and she clenched and unclenched her fists. I expected a floodgate to open, but she kept herself tightly under control and the orange gradually disappeared.

"When did you learn to relax like that?" I asked.

She smiled faintly. "I used to suffer from stress until I went to transcendental meditation classes. How do you know?"

"It was in your aura." I put down my yellow pencil and picked up the green. "Before I change colors, I'd better mention that you'd gain a great deal of pleasure out of some sort of creative hobby. For instance, you would get enormous satisfaction out of expressing yourself in some way, perhaps singing or writing."

She nodded. "I used to."

"You also have a great deal of green in your aura. This is interesting as it shows that deep down you are a caring person and you'd make a natural healer. You probably relate well to plants and animals, as well as people."

"Much better with animals than people." Again she gave a harsh, self-contemptuous laugh.

"The green harmonizes well with your pink ground color. You enjoy challenges and enjoy making your mark. You are prepared to work long and hard for whatever it is you want."

"I've always set goals for myself. Not that it's done me much good."

I shook my head. "Quite the opposite. It's just that you set goals for your career, but not for other areas of your life, such as relationships and family." The orange appeared again for several seconds, disappearing as quickly as it came. "That TM did you the world of good!"

She shifted uncomfortably. "I wouldn't want to live with you. You know too much."

I turned the drawing around to allow her to see what I had done. "Now I'm going to draw in the chakras. There are seven of these energy points in your body and they relate very much to your emotions and feelings about different areas of your life." I indicated where each one was located, and asked her to stand up for a moment. She appeared embarrassed as I looked at her chakras, and was relieved to sit down again.

I quickly drew in each chakra. "I'll go over these one by one, but as you'll see, they are all interconnected, and you have a number of blockages that are holding you back right now."

"Has that just happened?"

"It's probably a gradual buildup. However, it seems to me that you've reached a crisis point, and where you go from here is entirely up to you."

"I don't know where to go from here."

"Maybe this will give you some clues. Firstly, your root chakra is blocked. This chakra governs security and confidence. In fact, the Sanskrit word for it means 'support.' It keeps your feet on the ground. When it's blocked, as it is right now, you are likely to feel frightened or nervous or insecure."

"Insecure, I'd say. Frightened, maybe. Nervous? No."

"This chakra governs our fight or flight reflexes, so you may feel as if you want to run one minute, but stay and fight the next."

She nodded slowly. "That describes it exactly."

"Your sacral chakra is also blocked. When both the root and sacral chakras are blocked the problem often relates to sexual matters. It also means that you are probably expressing your feelings of resentment and anger."

"I'd like to express them, but I keep holding them back."

"You can't keep doing that. Look what it's doing to you! You need to find a safe way to get your feelings out into the open."

"Years ago I went to a secluded beach and shouted and screamed until I lost my voice."

"Did you feel better afterwards?"

She laughed, a natural, pleasant laugh this time. "It felt great until I turned around and saw my husband sitting on the sand behind me!"

"Maybe you should visit that beach again. Or maybe you should simply schedule a quiet intimate dinner so that you can quietly discuss what's on your mind—and heart."

"What makes you think it's my husband?"

"Well, it's not your career, that much is obvious. But it relates to your emotions on a very deep, almost primal level. My guess is that your husband won't say what's on his mind, or won't discuss the deeper things with you—"

"He's a bastard!"

"Maybe, but you still love him."

She leaned forward. "Does my aura say that?"

"I'm getting a bit ahead of myself, but your heart chakra is in perfect balance. That means that, despite everything, you still can love. The fact that it's balanced tends to indicate that he still loves you, too. However, I'd really have to see his aura to answer that properly."

"Jim loves me?" Surprise was evident in her voice. She reached out and touched me on the knee. "You really think he does?"

"I don't think it. But I can feel it and see it in your aura. You have a lot of love to give, too."

For the first time she smiled and it made her look ten years younger.

"I'll go back to your solar chakra now. This chakra is over-stimulated. You've become a perfectionist and a workaholic. You're probably very demanding on others."

She licked her lips and nodded. "I can change that."

"You heart chakra is in perfect balance, as I said before. This means that you are able to help and nurture others. With your compassion and love you can help build other people up and give them hope and strength."

"I should have done that with my family."

"You still can. It's never too late, and your family knows that you love them. It's impossible to hide the glow coming from your heart chakra."

"Thank you."

"Now we come to the top three chakras. They are known as the Trinity. Your throat chakra is slightly over-stimulated. You can express yourself wonderfully well, but right now you are probably feeling dogmatic, sarcastic and bitter. Once you release that, your communication with others will be excellent again.

"Your brow chakra is well balanced. It's surprising in some ways, because it relates to your thinking, and that seems a little confused right now. Basically, this chakra shows that whenever you're presented with a problem, you'll find the answer by using your excellent brain. It also shows that you have a fine intuition, and the potential to make much more use of it than you have in the past."

"I'm becoming more aware of that now. That's probably one reason I've come to see you."

"We have just one more chakra. This one's the crown chakra. It's reasonably well developed. I say 'reasonably,' because most people don't even start to work on this chakra until they are getting on a bit in life. You are basically in tune with the infinite, and will become more and more aware of your spiritual nature as time goes on.

"You have an area of blackness in your etheric body beside your right knee. This has been there a long while. Did you injure yourself there at some time?"

"I broke it as a teenager, playing hockey. I sometimes get twinges of arthritis from it now."

"Apart from that your health looks good, except for the strain going on right now. A vacation would do you the world of good, particularly if you went somewhere new, where you could look at your problems from a distance. You need to step outside yourself for a little bit and look at things from a different perspective. It would also restore your strength and vitality."

She nodded. "Not to mention my enthusiasm. I'm thinking of doing that. Thank you."

"There are a number of thought forms in your aura as well. The most pronounced of these are books. You obviously have a desire to learn right now."

"I'm planning to go back to college."

"Excellent. That's what the books mean. I can also see a rope with a large knot in it. This means that a major part of your life is in a mess and you need to untie the knot. I think we both know what area of your life that is."

She nodded her head thoughtfully. "Less work, more play. Is that what you recommend?"

"It's up to you, of course. But I think you need to get more balance into your life. You obviously love your work and are doing well at it, so keep on with it. Your career is extremely important to you. But it would be good if you could make a bit more room for the other important parts of your life. If you were able to take that vacation you'd have time to think about all of these things.

"In conclusion, I'd like to say that you have an extremely striking aura. You have been blessed with more ability and potential than most, and you are taking them as far as you can. Remember to take the special people in your life along with you. I see much success and great happiness in your future."

My longer aura readings can take up to an hour, depending on what is in the aura. In many ways, an

aura reader is a counselor, and it would help you enormously to attend counseling courses to develop your
skills in this area, if you wish to become a professional
aura reader.

This woman was not as communicative as most.
Usually, a reading becomes a conversation. I enjoy
people making comments and asking questions as I
give the reading. When people ask questions I am able
to look at different parts of the aura to find the answer.
I think this sort of reading is much more helpful than
the ones where the person sits quietly and simply lis-
tens. Sometimes these people are testing you and don't
want to give any clues, but usually, they are not aware
that they can ask questions. Consequently, I normally
begin by telling my clients that they can ask whatever
questions they wish as I proceed. When they do, you
can provide the information that is most likely to be
useful to them.

An aura reading is an extremely intimate experience for both the reader and the person being read.
People cannot hide anything from you. They might be
able to lie convincingly, but you will be able to see the
truth revealed in their auras. Many people have a need
to lie to try to bolster themselves up. I seldom question what they say when I see the opposite revealed in
their auras. But I bear it in mind when I am giving
them advice.

Aura reading can be very satisfying, particularly
when you see people growing and progressing as a
result of your advice. Start by giving extremely brief
readings. Ask your friends and acquaintances for feed-

back on your accuracy. You will find it is easy to find subjects to practice on. Once people hear that you are giving aura readings they will seek you out. As you learn more and become better and better, expand the length of your readings. The aura readings I give as an "entertainment" take about five minutes and skim quickly over the surface. However, a full aura reading often takes an hour.

Giving readings can be very draining emotionally. It is important that you release any negative thoughts and emotions that you accidentally pick up from the people you read for. I find it helpful to close my eyes and take several deep breaths after a long reading. As I exhale, I say to myself, "relax and let go." Finally, I imagine myself surrounded with an aura of protection. By doing this I can give readings all day long and still feel fresh and energetic at the end of the day.

It is important to protect yourself in this way. Some people will tell you extremely tragic and sad stories. Their negativity and bitterness can attach itself to you, dragging you down and depleting your energies. You owe it to yourself, and the people you read for, to keep a positive outlook and stay in good health, so that you can help everyone who comes to you to the best of your ability.

You also need to learn how to be concerned and caring, but detached at the same time. This is similar to the feelings that doctors and nurses must learn. You cannot become emotionally involved with your clients' problems. You need to be an empathetic humanitarian to become a successful reader, but you must not allow other people's problems to become yours. Your duty is to help other people as much as you can, but to look after yourself as well.

If you do this you will be able to help many people. It is a wonderful feeling when people come up to you, sometimes years after having a reading, to say how much you helped them. Aura reading can be highly rewarding in many different ways.

Conclusion

As you become more and more aware of auras your life will change permanently. You will become much more interested in colors than ever before. You will see so much more beauty in the world and will wonder how you missed seeing it in the past. The study of auras is a fascinating interest that can expand your awareness of the world and enable you to help others as well as yourself.

Be aware that there are many misconceptions about auras. You will be misunderstood at times. Some people regard auras as a hallucination. Others feel it is the work of the devil. Of course, still others think it is the work of God. You will find that some people think that you see auras around everyone, all the time. Some people will feel that it gives you an unfair advantage over others.

Be gentle with the people who scoff at your ability to see and read auras. In time, if not in this incarnation, in another one, they will discover the truth about auras.

May your life be filled to profusion with all the colors of the rainbow.

Appendix A:
Meanings of the Colors

You will find an enormous range of colors inside people's auras. The sheer variety may seem daunting at first, but as you gain experience you will find it easier than you think to interpret the colors.

Fortunately, over the last few thousand years, many people have studied auras and there is agreement about what the different colors mean. It is easy, for example, to recognize that a dirty, dark red color indicates a bad temper and sensuality, but it may not be as simple to interpret a bright maroon or a washed-out rose color.

This list is intended as a guide only. It has been compiled from my findings as well as that of my students. Trust your intuition and make up your own mind about any unusual colors you see before checking them with this list. You may find that you disagree with the basic meaning shown here. When this happens, look at the color again to make sure that it agrees with the description given. In cases of doubt, follow your intuition.

I debated about including this list, as it is better for you to discover the meanings for yourself by observation and by asking questions. However, in my classes, I found that most people want something to confirm their findings. Consequently, use this as a guide, but stop using it as soon as you become comfortable and familiar with the different colors you find.

Speaking generally, clear, beautiful colors are always a positive sign, while dirty looking colors are invariably negative.

Most of the colors listed here appear as thought forms and come and go rapidly. When emotion is attached they will stay much longer. With practice you will learn which colors are part of the permanent aura and which ones come and go according to the changing moods and feelings of the people you deal with.

RED: energy

Blood red: vengefulness and jealousy
Bright red: force and persuasion
Clear red: friendliness and physical activity
Crimson: sexuality and base passions
Dark red, almost black: selfishness and greed
Deep red: passion
Dirty red: sensuality and lust
Dull red: selfishness

Fiery red: irritability and anxiety
Light red: nervousness
Magenta: cheerfulness
Rose: pure, unselfish love
Rose-pink: joy and happiness
Scarlet: uncontrollable emotions
True red: ambition and courage

ORANGE: emotions

Bright orange: strong emotions
Clear orange: sociability and openness
Dark orange: over-indulgence, lack of emotional control
Dull orange: irritability
Reddish orange: desire to impress others
True orange: well organized and competent

YELLOW: intellect

Bright yellow: high intellect
Dull yellow: laziness and impracticality
Lemon yellow: clear thinking
Mustard yellow: craftiness and dishonesty
Pale yellow: thoughtfulness
Luminous yellow: good logic and spiritual aspirations
True yellow: sociable, communicative and thoughtful
Yellow-green: low intellect

GREEN: healing and balance

Bright green: good health and vitality
Dark green: jealousy
Dirty green: envy, dishonesty and deceit
Emerald green: empathy

Grass green: adaptability
Grayish green: depression and disillusionment
Light green: sympathy, understanding and forgiveness
Muddy green: envy
True green: humanistic and kind-hearted

BLUE: variety

Bright blue: self-reliance and loyalty
Dark blue: wisdom
Dull blue: feelings of being restricted and held back
Light blue: devotion and high ideals
Lilac-blue: idealism
Pale blue: immaturity
Rich blue: spirituality
True blue: imaginative and perceptive

INDIGO: responsibility

Bright indigo: concern for others
Dark indigo: spiritual awareness
Dull indigo: disillusion
Luminous indigo: serenity
True indigo: self-reliant and responsible

VIOLET: spirituality

Amethyst: spiritual awakening
Lilac: humanitarian
Luminous violet: faith, intuition and awareness
Purple: pride and love of pomp and ceremony
True violet: intuitive and spiritual

BLACK: malice

Grayish black: malevolence and cruelty
Pure black in the etheric body: health problems.
Can also indicate pain. Hatred and viciousness
when found elsewhere
True black: strong-willed and opinionated
Washed-out black: secretiveness and pessimism

BROWN: materialism

Dirty brown: miserliness
Muddy brown: selfishness
Pure brown: ambition and materialism
Reddish brown: greed
True brown: down-to-earth and hard-working

GOLD: wisdom

Clear gold: good intellect and ability to impart
knowledge to others
Luminous gold: positivity and support for others
True gold: idealistic and principled
Yellow-gold: contentment and physical well-being

GRAY: conventionality

Bright gray: selfishness and lack of imagination
Dull gray: boredom, fear and melancholy
Greenish gray: negative thinking
Gray around the head: headache
Grayish brown: ill health
Gray smudge in etheric body: beginning of an illness

Lead gray: self-doubt
Light gray: ill health and lack of energy
True gray: stressed and burned out

PINK: love

Clear pink: compassion
Coral pink: uncertainty and immaturity
Pure pink: tenderness and devotion
Rose-pink: joyfulness and optimism
Salmon pink: humanitarianism and universal love
True pink: affectionate, loving and sympathetic
Washed-out pink: dependence

SILVER: idealism

Bright silver: romantic and trustworthy
Dull silver: idealistic dreamer
True silver: honorable and honest

WHITE: purity

Creamy white: humanitarianism and idealism
Luminous white: perfection and spiritual awareness
True white: perfectionist

Appendix B:
Keywords for the Chakras

Root Chakra

POSITIVE	NEGATIVE
Active	Dominating
Ambitious	Egotistical
Confident	Self-centered
Determined	Stubborn
Sexual	Sensual
Spontaneous	Impulsive

Sacral Chakra

POSITIVE	NEGATIVE
Adaptable	Apathetic
Ambitious	Indifferent
Cooperative	Selfish
Diplomatic	Manipulative
Friendly	Timid
Honest	Superficial
Hospitable	Overly Sensitive

Solar Chakra

POSITIVE	NEGATIVE
Analytical	Critical
Charming	Superficial
Creative	Dilettante
Eloquent	Frivolous
Enthusiastic	Moody
Flexible	Contradictory
Inspirational	Trivial

Heart Chakra

POSITIVE	NEGATIVE
Compassionate	Selfish
Faithful	Insecure
Generous	Limited
Nurturing	Dominating
Open-hearted	Mistrustful
Persevering	Frustrated
Serious	Rigid
Sincere	Stubborn

Throat Chakra

POSITIVE	NEGATIVE
Adaptable	Erratic
Enthusiastic	Hesitant
Idealistic	Impatient
Loyal	Authoritarian
Peaceful	Restless
Progressive	Over-indulgent

Brow Chakra

POSITIVE	NEGATIVE
Aesthetic	Exacting
Friendly	Fearful
Generous	Critical
Inspired	Overwhelmed
Intuitive	Forgetful
Loving	Fussy
Understanding	Interfering

Crown Chakra

POSITIVE	NEGATIVE
Charming	Introverted
Creative	Negative
Intuitive	Introspective
Logical	Critical
Mystical	Daydreamer
Peaceful	Self-centered
Poised	Isolated
Transforming	Intolerant

Notes

Introduction

1. *The Human Aura* by Winifred G. Barton, Psi-Science Productions, Ottawa, Canada, n.d., page 5.

2. *The Jerusalem Bible*, Darton, Longman and Todd Limited, London, 1966, page 122 (Exodus 34:29).

3. *The Human Aura* by Wifred G. Barton, page 25.

4. *A Layman's Guide to New Age and Spiritual Terms* by Elaine Murray, Blue Dolphin Publishing, Inc., Nevada City, 1993, page 25.

5. *The Occult Explosion* by Nat Freedland, G. P. Putnam's Sons, New York, 1972. Reprinted by Berkley Publishing Corporation, New York, 1972, page 23.

6. *Encyclopaedia of Psychic Science* by Nandor Fodor, University Books, Inc., New York, 1966, page 17.

7. *The Human Aura,* edited by Nicholas Regush, Berkley Books, New York, 1977, page 1.

8. *The Human Aura,* edited by Nicholas Regush, page 24.

9. *Handbook of Psi Discoveries* by Sheila Ostrander and Lynn Schroeder, Sphere Books Limited, London, 1977, page 203. This book also contains several of Baron von Reichenbach's experiments.

10. *The Human Aura,* edited by Nicholas Regush, page 33.

11. *The Human Atmosphere* by W. J. Kilner, MA, MB, ChB, MRCP, Kegan Paul, Trench, Trubner & Company, London, 1920.

12. *Electrical Coronas* by L. B. Loeb, University of California Press, 1965, pages 23–37. The corona effect is the electrical phenomenon that causes the Aurora Borealis, and the effect known as St. Elmo's fire where glowing balls of light are sometimes seen during thunderstorms.

13. *Psychic Discoveries Behind the Iron Curtain* by Sheila Ostrander and Lynn Schroeder, Bantam Books, New York, 1971, page 227.

14. *A Layman's Guide to New Age and Spiritual Terms* by Elaine Murray, page 28.

15. *Everyone Is Psychic* by Elizabeth Fuller, Crown Publishers, Inc., New York, 1989, page 154.

Chapter One

1. *The Human Aura,* edited by Nicholas Regush, Berkley Books, New York, 1977. Article by Dr Charles Tart called "The Scientific Study of the Human Aura," page 141. Originally published in *Journal of the Society for Psychical Research*, 46:751, 1972.

2. Red light has a wavelength of 0.8µ, while violet has 0.4µ (a micron is 1/1000 of a millimeter).

3. *Color and Music in the New Age* by Corinne Heline, DeVorss and Company, Marina del Rey, 1964, page 40.

4. *From Copernicus to Einstein* by Hans Reichenbach, Philosophical Library, New York, 1942. My edition is published by Dover Publications, Inc., New York, 1980, page 31.

5. *New Idea*, November 2, 1985, pages 69–71. Unattributed article titled "Moody Blues . . . and Yellows."

6. *Occult Illustrated Dictionary* by Harvey Day, Kaye and Ward Ltd., London, 1975, page 14. (Also published in the United States by Oxford University Press Inc., New York, 1976.)

7. The three layers are the Mental Aura, Astral Aura and Spiritual Aura. The spiritual aura surrounds the other layers and the degree of spirituality of the person is revealed by the coloration and size of this layer of the aura. Lord Gautama Buddha had an aura that was said to extend several miles. Jesus' aura was even larger. St. Paul wrote: "In Him we live and move and have our being." (Acts of the Apostles, chapter 17, verse 28.)

8. *How to read the Aura* by W. E. Butler, Aquarian Press, Wellingborough, 1971. Revised edition published 1979 by Aquarian Press and Samuel Weiser, Inc., York Beach, page 16.

9. *The Mystery of the Human Aura* by Ursula Roberts, The Spiritualist Association of Great Britain, London, 1950. Revised edition published 1984 by Samuel Weiser, Inc., York Beach, page 7.

Chapter Two

1. *The Healing Power of Colour* by Betty Wood, The Aquarian Press, Wellingborough, 1984, page 71.

2. *Dowsing for Beginners* by Richard Webster, Llewellyn Publications, St. Paul, 1996.

3. *Dowsing for Beginners* by Richard Webster. Pages 13–20.

4. *The Human Aura* edited by Nicholas Regush. Article by Dr. Charles T. Tart called "The Scientific Study of the Human Aura," pages 145–150.

Chapter Three

1. An exercise to assist you in seeing your own aura is described in *Handbook of Psi Discoveries* by Sheila Ostrander and Lynn Schroeder, originally published in 1974. My edition was published by Sphere Books Limited, London in 1977. Page 73.

Chapter Four

1. Reenu Boyatzis, "Children's Emotional Associations with Colors." Article in *Journal of Genetic Psychology*, Vol. 155, March 1994, page 77.

2. R. S. Cimbalo, K. L. Beck and D. S. Sendziak, "Emotional Toned Pictures and Color Selection for Children and College Students." Article in *The Journal of Genetic Psychology*, Vol. 133, 1978, pages 303–304.

3. Elaine Murray, *A Layman's Guide to New Age and Spiritual Terms*, page 28.

4. *New Idea*, November 2, 1985, page 69.

5. The color and number combinations shown here are the standard ones, and I have found them extremely accurate. However, a number of people have come up with different combinations. An example is Barbara J.

Bishop, who gives the following combinations in her book *Numerology: The Universal Vibrations of Numbers* (Llewellyn Publications, St. Paul, 1990): 1 = red, 2 = orange, 3 = yellow, 4 = green, 5 = blue, 6 = purple, 7 = black, 8 = gray and 9 = white. Experiment, and see which particular combinations work for you.

6. *Talisman Magic* by Richard Webster, Llewellyn Publications, St. Paul, 1995, page 56.

7. *Psychic Phenomena* by Dr. Joe H. Slate, McFarland and Company, Inc., Jefferson, 1988, page 70.

Chapter Five

1. *The Magician's Companion* by Bill Whitcomb, Llewellyn Publications, St. Paul, 1993, page 101.

2. *Science and the Evolution of Consciousness: Chakras, Ki, and Psi* by Dr. Hiroshi Motoyama and R. Brown, Autumn Press, Inc., Brookline, 1978, pages 93–98.

3. *Vibrational Medicine* by Richard Gerber, M.D., Bear and Company Publishing, Santa Fe, 1988, page 132.

4. *Vibrational Medicine* by Richard Gerber, M.D., page 133. Dr. Valerie Hunt's original findings were recorded in her article "Electronic Evidence of Auras, Chakras in UCLA Study" in *Brain/Mind Bulletin*, Vol. 3, no. 9 (March 20, 1978). Dr. Hunt found that the normal frequencies of brain waves were between 0 and 100 cycles per second. Muscle frequency was up to 225 cps, and the heart 250 cps. However, the readings over the chakras lay in a range of frequencies between 100 and 1600 cps.

5. *Vibrational Medicine* by Richard Gerber, M.D., pages 133–134.

6. *Omens, Oghams & Oracles* by Richard Webster, Llewellyn Publications, St. Paul, 1995, page 14.

Chapter Six

1. According to the British Color Council there are 1,400 shades of blue, 1,375 shades of brown, 1,000 reds, 820 greens, 550 oranges, 500 grays, 360 violets and 12 whites. *The Aura and What It Means to You*, a compilation from many authorities, published by Health Research, Molelumne Hill, n.d., page 4.

Chapter Seven

1. *ESP: The Sixth Sense* by Brian Ward, Macdonald Educational Limited, London, 1980, page 60. An American edition was published by Ideals Publishing Corporation, Milwaukee.

2. *ESP: The Sixth Sense* by Brian Ward, page 59.

3. *A Priest and the Paranormal* by Jack Dover Wellman, Churchman Publishing Ltd., Worthing, 1988, pages 166 and 167.

4. *The Human Aura* by Swami Panchadasi, Yoga Publication Society, Chicago, 1915.

5. *The Human Aura* by Swami Panchadasi. Also quoted in *Color Psychology and Color Therapy* by Faber Birren, Citadel Press, Secaucus, 1950. Revised edition, 1961. Pages 46–47.

6. *The Ancient Art of Color Therapy* by Linda A. Clark, The Devin-Adair Company, Old Greenwich, 1975, page 120.

7. *Color and Crystals* by Joy Gardner, The Crossing Press, Freedom, 1988, page 136.

8. *Colour Healing* by Mary Anderson, The Aquarian Press, Wellingborough, 1975. Revised second edition, 1979, page 73.

9. *Color and Personality* by Audrey Kargere, Philosophical Library, Inc., New York, 1949. Republished by Samuel Weiser, Inc., York Beach, 1979, page 64.

10. *Psychic Empowerment for Health and Fitness* by Dr. Joe H. Slate, Llewellyn Publications, St. Paul, 1996, pages 51–52.

11. *The Ancient Art of Color Therapy* by Linda A. Clark, page 121.

12. *Color and Music in the New Age* by Corinne Heline, page 44.

Chapter Eight

1. *Omens, Oghams & Oracles* by Richard Webster, Llewellyn Publications, St. Paul, 1995, pages 39–41. An oracle tree is a Celtic idea. You find a tree that relates well to you by hugging trees until you find one that responds to your touch. You can meditate under this tree, perform divination, and get in tune with yourself and the entire universe. By accepting the tree as your oracle tree you also accept the responsibility for looking after it and for its immediate surroundings.

2. *The Healing Energies of Music* by Hal A. Lingerman, The Theosophical Publishing House, Wheaton, 1983, page 60.

3. *The Healing Energies of Music* by Hal A. Lingerman, page 14.

4. *Your Body Doesn't Lie* by Dr. John Diamond, Warner Books, New York, 1980, page 98. Originally published as *BK, Behavioral Kinesiology* by Harper and Row, New York, 1979.

5. *Methods of Psychic Development* by Dr. Quantz Crawford, Samuel Weiser, Inc., York Beach, 1982, pages 89–90.

6. *Psychic Phenomena* by Dr. Joe H. Slate, page 74.

Glossary

ASTRAL BODY The astral body (sometimes known as astral double or emotional body) completely surrounds the physical body, and is composed of ethereal matter. Yogis believe that the soul dwells in the astral body.

AURA The aura is an invisible energy field that surrounds all living things. It not only surrounds the entire body, but is also part of every cell of the body and reflects all the subtle life energies. Consequently, it should be considered as an extension of the body, rather than something that surrounds it. Auras vary in size and coloration depending on the well-being and spiritual development of the person.

AURA PENDULUM The aura pendulum is a pendulum that contains the seven colors of the rainbow and a small indicator. The indicator marks the particular color that the person using it is working with at the time. It is commonly used by color therapists and chakra healers.

171

CHAKRAS The chakras are nerve centers of energy located along the spinal column in the etheric body. They absorb and distribute physical, mental, emotional and spiritual energies. The chakras are powerhouses of energy and, consequently, our personal electromagnetic energy is much greater at these points.

There are seven chakras:
1. *Root chakra*, at the base of the spine.
2. *Sacral chakra*, halfway between the pubic bone and the navel.
3. *Solar chakra*, at the level of the solar plexus.
4. *Heart chakra*, between the shoulder blades in line with the heart.
5. *Throat chakra*, at the level of the throat.
6. *Brow chakra*, at the level of the forehead, just above the eyebrows.
7. *Crown chakra*, at the top of the head.

COLOR BREATHING Color breathing is an exercise that brings the different colors of the rainbow into the body.

DOWSING Dowsing is a method of locating things, usually something that is hidden below the surface of the earth. Water divining is a good example. However, it can be used for many other purposes, such as dowsing for a person's aura.

EMOTIONAL BODY See **ASTRAL BODY**

ETHERIC BODY The etheric body duplicates the physical body and is believed to provide the physical body with energy and a sense of consciousness. It can move about in space for short periods of time away from the physical body. The church refers to it as *bilocation*, and a famous example of it occurred in Limoges, France, in 1226. St. Anthony of Padua was conducting a service there when he suddenly remembered that he was supposed to be preaching at the other end of town. He knelt down and drew his hood over his body while the congregation waited. At the same moment he was seen by monks at the other end of town reading a lesson from the Bible.

ETHERIC DOUBLE The etheric double is an extremely fine, almost invisible surround that extends between a quarter and half an inch all around the body. It expands during sleep and contracts during the waking hours. When people first develop auric sight they usually see the etheric double as a space between the physical body and the aura proper. However, as their sight develops they become aware that the etheric double has a grayish tinge that creates a wide variety of almost luminous colors that are constantly changing. The etheric double is sometimes known as the health aura, as illnesses can be seen here as a dark smudge or a break in the movements of the aura. Ill health can also be determined by a loss of coloration in the etheric double.

GROUND COLOR The ground color is the basic background color of the aura and is usually the first part of the aura that is seen by people when they first gain auric sight. This color reveals what the person should be doing with his or her life. People who are completely fulfilled have large, vibrant ground colors, in contrast to the small, pale ground colors of people who have no idea where they are going.

HALO In religious art, holy people are often shown with a luminous or golden surround around their heads. These are partial depictions of an aura and are known as halos. They have been known from well before Christian times.

HEALTH AURA See **ETHERIC DOUBLE**

KIRLIAN PHOTOGRAPHY A system of photographing the energy fields around all living things. It was discovered, by accident, by Semyon and Valentina Kirlian in the 1930s.

LAYERS OF THE AURA See **SUBTLE BODIES**

MOOD AURA The ground color can be replaced temporarily by other colors as our moods change. The mood aura reflects our emotional state. If, for example, you were enjoying a pleasant day and someone suddenly insulted you, your aura would respond to reflect the sudden change in your emotional state. This color would be more visible than your usual aura colors, until you were able to let go of the emotions.

PHYSICAL AURA The physical aura is made up of the physical matter and energy fields that surround the body. Because we are usually warm in relation to our surroundings, we all have thermal gradients which create air currents close to our bodies. Infrared energy is constantly radiated from our bodies. We also have electrostatic and electrical ion fields surrounding us. Also, we emit low levels of electromagnetic radiation (radio waves) and low frequency radiation of as much as one hundred kilocycles.

PSYCHIC VAMPIRE Psychic vampires are people who drain other people's auric energy to enhance their own. This can be done consciously or unconsciously.

QUATERN The four bottom chakras are often referred to as the quatern, and are depicted as a square.

RADIATING COLORS These are colors inside the aura that radiate outwards from the body.

SUBTLE BODIES Auras consist of different layers known as subtle bodies. Most people who can see auras are able to see at least three. However, some people are able to identify and see all seven of the different layers that make up the aura. These are:
1. The Physical Etheric Plane
2. The Astral Plane
3. The Lower Mental Plane
4. The Higher Mental Plane

5. The Spiritual Plane
6. The Intuitional Plane
7. The Absolute Plane

THOUGHT FORMS Our thoughts can become temporarily visible inside the aura, particularly if there is a degree of emotion attached to them. These are known as thought forms.

TRINITY The top three chakras are often referred to as the trinity or triad. These chakras vibrate at a higher level than the lower four chakras.

Suggested Reading

Anderson, Mary. *Colour Healing*. Wellingborough: The Aquarian Press, 1975. Revised edition 1979.

Andrews, Ted. *How to See and Read the Aura*. St. Paul, MN: Llewellyn Publications, 1991.

Bagnall, Oscar. *The Origins and Properties of the Human Aura*. New York: University Books, Inc., 1970.

Baker, Dr. Douglas. *The Human Aura*. Dr. Douglas Baker, Essenden, 1986.

Barton, Winifred. *The Human Aura*. Ottawa: Psi-Science Productions Ltd., 1973.

Bendit, Lawrence J., and Phoebe D. Bendit. *The Etheric Body of Man*. Wheaton: The Theosophical Publishing House, 1977.

Besant, Annie, and C.W. Leadbeater, *Thought-Forms*. Wheaton: The Theosophical Publishing House, 1925. Abridged edition 1969.

Birren, Faber. *Color and Human Response*. New York: Van Nostrand Reinhold, 1978.

Birren, Faber. *Color Psychology and Color Therapy*. Secaucus: The Citadel Press, 1950.

Breaux, Charles. *Journey into Consciousness*. York Beach: Nicolas-Hays, Inc., 1989.

Brennan, Barbara Ann. *Hands of Light: A Guide to Healing Through the Human Energy Field*. New York: Bantam New Age, 1987.

Brennan, Barbara Ann. *Light Emerging*. New York: Bantam New Age, 1993.

Butler, W. E. *How to Read the Aura*. Wellingborough: The Aquarian Press, 1971. Revised edition 1979.

Cayce, Edgar. *Auras*. Virginia Beach: A. R. E. Press, 1945.

Dale, Cyndi. *New Chakra Healing*. St. Paul, MN: Llewellyn Publications, 1996.

David, William. *The Harmonics of Sound, Color and Vibration*. Marina del Rey: DeVorss and Co., 1980.

Diamond, Dr. John. *Life Energy: Unlocking the Hidden Power of Your Emotions to Achieve Total Well-Being*. New York: Dodd, Mead and Co., 1985.

Diamond, Dr. John. *Your Body Doesn't Lie*. New York: Warner Books, 1980. Originally published as *BK, Behavioral Kinesiology* by Harper and Row, New York, 1979.

Don, Frank. *Color Your World*. New York: Destiny Books, 1977.

Gerber, Dr. Richard. *Vibrational Medicine*. Santa Fe: Bear and Company, 1988.

Gregory, Laneta, and Geoffrey Treissman. *Handbook of the Aura*. Tasburgh: Pilgrims Book Services, 1985.

Health Research (compilation). *The Aura and What It Means to You*. Health Research, Mokelumne Hill, 1956.

Hills, Norah (editor). *You are a Rainbow*. Boulder Creek: University of the Trees Press, 1979.

Hodson, Geoffrey. *The Seven Human Temperaments*. Adyar: The Theosophical Publishing House, 1952.

Iovine, John. *Kirlian Photography: A Hands-On Guide*. Blue Ridge Summit: Tab Books Inc., 1994.

Jaegers, Bevy. *Secrets of the Aura*. Cottonwood: Esoteric Publications, 1978.

Karagulla, Shafica. *Breakthrough to Creativity*. Santa Monica: DeVorss and Co., 1967.

Kargere, Audrey. *Color and Personality*. York Beach: Samuel Weiser, Inc., 1979. Originally published by Philosophical Library Inc., 1949.

Kent, Win. *The Living Power of Colour*. London: The International Association of Colour Healers, n.d.

Kilner, Walter J. *The Aura*. York Beach: Samuel Weiser, Inc., 1973.

Leadbeater, Charles W. *Man, Visible and Invisible*. Adyar: The Theosophical Publishing House, 1925.

Leadbeater, Charles W. *The Chakras*. Wheaton: The Theosophical Publishing House, 1972.

Leadbeater, Charles W. *The Inner Life*. Wheaton: The Theosophical Publishing House, 1978.

Lingerman, Hal A. *The Healing Energies of Music*. Wheaton: The Theosophical Publishing House, 1983.

Mella, Dorothee L. *The Language of Color.* New York: Viking Penguin Inc., 1988.

Muftic, Mahmoud K. *Researches on the Aura Phenomena.* Hastings: The Society of Metaphysicians, 1970.

Ostram, Joseph. *Understanding Auras.* London: Harper Collins, 1993. (Originally published as *You and Your Aura*, 1987.)

Ouseley, S. G. J. *Science of the Aura.* London: L. N. Fowler and Co. Ltd., 1949.

Panchadasi, Swami. *The Human Aura: Astral Colours and Thought Forms.* Hackensack: Wehman Brothers, 1940.

Powell, Arthur. *The Etheric Double.* London: The Theosophical Publishing House, 1969.

Regush, Nicholas (editor). *The Human Aura.* New York: Berkley Books, 1977.

Rendel, Peter. *Introduction to the Chakras.* Wellingborough: The Aquarian Press, 1974. Revised edition 1979.

Roberts, Ursula. *The Mystery of the Human Aura.* York Beach: Samuel Weiser, Inc., 1977. Revised edition 1984. (Originally published by The Spiritualist Association of Great Britain, London, 1950.)

Slate, Dr. Joe H. *Psychic Empowerment for Health and Fitness.* St. Paul, MN: Llewellyn Publications, 1996.

Smith, Mark. *Auras—See Them in Only 60 Seconds!* St. Paul, MN: Llewellyn Publications, 1997.

Whyman, Earl Monteith. *Colour for Health.* Heretaunga Park: Practitioner Skills Limited, 1992.

Wood, Betty. *The Healing Power of Colour.* Wellingborough: The Aquarian Press, 1984.

Index

☾ LOOK FOR THE CRESCENT MOON

Llewellyn publishes hundreds of books on your favorite subjects! To get these exciting books, including the ones on the following pages, check your local bookstore or order them directly from Llewellyn.

ORDER BY PHONE

- Call toll-free within the U.S. and Canada, 1-800-THE MOON
- In Minnesota, call (612) 291-1970
- We accept VISA, MasterCard, and American Express

ORDER BY MAIL

- Send the full price of your order (MN residents add 7% sales tax) in U.S. funds, plus postage & handling to:

  Llewellyn Worldwide
  P.O. Box 64383, Dept. K798-6
  St. Paul, MN 55164–0383, U.S.A.

POSTAGE & HANDLING

(For the U.S., Canada, and Mexico)
- $4.00 for orders $15.00 and under
- $5.00 for orders over $15.00
- No charge for orders over $100.00

We ship UPS in the continental United States. We ship standard mail to P.O. boxes. Orders shipped to Alaska, Hawaii, The Virgin Islands, and Puerto Rico are sent first-class mail. Orders shipped to Canada and Mexico are sent surface mail.

International orders: Airmail—add freight equal to price of each book to the total price of order, plus $5.00 for each non-book item (audio tapes, etc.).

Surface mail—Add $1.00 per item.

Allow 4–6 weeks for delivery on all orders.
Postage and handling rates subject to change.

DISCOUNTS

We offer a 20% discount to group leaders or agents. You must order a minimum of 5 copies of the same book to get our special quantity price.

FREE CATALOG

Get a free copy of our color catalog, *New Worlds of Mind and Spirit*. Subscribe for just $10.00 in the United States and Canada ($30.00 overseas, airmail). Many bookstores carry *New Worlds*—ask for it!

Visit our web site at www.llewellyn.com for more information.

Seven Secrets to Success
A Story of Hope
Richard Webster

Originally written as a letter from the author to his suicidal friend, this inspiring little book has been photocopied, passed along from person to person, and even appeared on the internet without the author's permission. Now available in book form, this underground classic offers hope to the weary and motivation for us all to let go of the past and follow our dreams.

It is the story of Kevin, who at the age of twenty-eight is on the verge of suicide after the failure of his business and his marriage. Then he meets Todd Melvin, an elderly gentleman with a mysterious past. As their friendship unfolds, Todd teaches Kevin seven secrets—secrets that can give you the power to turn your life around, begin anew, and reap success beyond your wildest dreams.

1-56718-797-8, 5 ³⁄₁₆ x 8, 144 pp., softcover $6.95

To order, call 1-800-THE-MOON
Prices subject to change without notice